Author's

After six years' service in the _____ . ____ the war, Bernard Benjamin completed his first degree, in English, and started teaching. He was subsequently Headmaster of four secondary schools in London, Essex and Cheshire. The last two schools were special schools for pupils with behaviour and learning handicaps. He was awarded an M.A. degree in Literature and a M.Ed. degree for research into the self-image of handicapped pupils.

BENJAMIN'S EXERCISES IN ENGLISH GRAMMAR

Bernard Benjamin

SPHERE BOOKS LTD

A *Sphere* Book

First published in Great Britain by Sphere Books Ltd 1991

Typeset by 🅰 Tek Art Ltd, Addiscombe, Croydon, Surrey
Printed and bound in Great Britain at The Guernsey Press

ISBN 0 7474 0994 3

Sphere Books Limited
A Division of
Macdonald & Co (Publishers) Ltd
165 Great Dover Street
London SE1 4YA

A member of Maxwell Macmillan Publishing Corporation

I dedicate this manual to all my friends
from whose mistakes I have
learnt so much.

Contents

PART I:
ELEMENTARY EXERCISES

The exercises in this section offer opportunities to revise your knowledge of the functions of the parts of speech.

The varied examples of parsing are designed to explore the eight basic relationships.

Nouns

The noun is the **naming** word. It is ubiquitous, and few sentences exist without containing one or more nouns.

<u>Remember</u>

Kind: common, proper, collective, abstract

Gender: masculine, feminine, common, neuter

Number: singular, plural

Note: The **case** of nouns is dealt with at the start of Part II.

Exercise 1
Each of these phrases contains a noun. What **kind** is it?

the silly boy, a black eye, is that Scotland? a brave horsewoman, his blindness, my poor feet, the gun-carrier, an assembly, my Rolls-Royce, his honesty, your pencil, that bunch of grapes, this group, the athlete, I saw Prince Charles, a black beetle, who killed Cock Robin? his great knowledge, the team lost, a dead rabbit.

Exercise 2
Each of these phrases contain two nouns. What **kind** are they?

a film-star called Roger Moore, a herd of cattle, a bottle of sauce, two pounds of sugar, the city of

Rome, a mob of soldiers, my friend Billy, a chair for the professor, a school for girls, the sweetness of honey, give a thought for the dog, a ship of the fleet, Alexander the Great showed much bravery, a postman called John, two boxes of matches, a lion in Chester Zoo, my sense of smell, a pint of milk, a mountain on the moon, a change of clothing.

Comment

'boxes' – Although these are 'collections' of matches, this is a **common** noun.

'change' – **common** noun.

Exercise 3

Give the **gender** and **number** of these nouns:

mother, child, tables, trousers, person, matron, books, scouts, wine, lady, saucers, Arab, candlestick, ram, Dane, folk, bricks, Jimmy Carter, father, Japanese.

Comment

'trousers' – is a **plural** word.

'folk' – It is possible to speak of 'a folk', but the word is normally **plural**.

Exercise 4

Give the **gender** and **number** of the nouns in these sentences and say what **kind** they are.

Father gave Robert two bars of chocolate for his lunch.

When Sheila was young, her sister held her hand when they went to school.

An idea occurred to the class: the captain of the team should wear a special badge.

Henry VIII had six wives but only one son.
Helen found a clutch of blackbird's eggs in a tree near her home.
The ghost of a child appeared near the window.
Crowds of coal-miners and their wives went to the meeting at Sheffield.
The tigers hid their cubs in the undergrowth when the natives attacked.
Louis XVI and Marie Antoinette were beheaded by the French mob at the Bastille during the Revolution.

Comment

'class' and 'team' – are **collective** nouns.

'ghost' – Gender? Normally this could be in the eye of the beholder, but linked with 'child', it should be **common**.

'French' – Adjective here, of course.

Pronouns

On the heels of the noun comes the pronoun, the word that takes its place. With these useful words, a book becomes 'it', a postman becomes 'he', a woman 'she', those boys over there 'them'. Other non-specific words appear: 'that' – an object we point to in the distance; 'some' – an undefined number of things on the table. Relatives can be seen not as cousins or uncles but the person 'who'; an article as 'which'. We find ourselves enquiring 'what?' and are shown the 'one' our friend had in mind. We are in the land of pronouns.

Remember

Kind: personal, demonstrative, relative, interrogative

Gender: masculine, feminine, common, neuter

Number: singular, plural

Person: 1st, 2nd, 3rd

Exercise 5
State the **kind** of pronoun used in these sentences. (The figure tells you how many there are in each sentence.)

I gave him the book. (2)
That is not yours. (2)
One of them said you sent him home. (4)
The coat that I found was hers. (2)
Which did you choose? (2)

Thou shalt not kill. (1)

We were late because of them. (2)

Those are ripe, you can eat some of them. (4)

Don't let him touch that, it is poison. (3)

Whose is this? (3)

The policeman arrested the man who was later charged. (1)

What did the teacher want me for? (2)

Exercise 6
Do the same in these sentences, and say if the 36 pronouns are **singular** or **plural**.

They were asleep and made me wait while they dressed. (3)

This is what I shall wear when he comes for tea. (4)

Give him those for me and make sure you get a receipt. (4)

It seems cold today; I shall wear your coat, if you don't mind. (3)

The singer wondered who was playing the piano; it sounded out of tune. (2)

This is the clock which my father made when he was just twenty. (3)

Which do you like, the green one or the blue one? (4)

They gave us a fright, firing like that. (3)

He must like her very much, to have asked her to marry him. (4)

It's the girl who told me all about you; she's the one. (6)

Comment
Watch 'your' coat and 'my' father = adjectives.

Exercise 7
Give the **person** of each of the pronouns in italics, and say which **gender** it is.

I sold *it* to *you* yesterday.
Did *they* call *him* last night?
She told *me* it was *yours*.
You ran away from *us* when *they* arrived.
Will *I* see *them* tomorrow?
It doesn't belong to *her*, but to *you*.
We tried to reach *it* before *they* got there.
Can *you* come to see *me* tomorrow?
They told *us* it would be too late for *you* and for *her*
　　to join the *others*.

Adjectives

The adjective dances close attendance on its noun or pronoun, and cannot really exist without it. No sooner does the noun appear than the adjective is by its side, defining, describing, enumerating, questioning. It registers the intensity of the description on a scale of three, adding colour and definition to the austere noun.

Remember

Kind: descriptive, possessive, proper, quantitative, numeral, demonstrative, interrogative, distributive

Degree: positive, comparative, superlative

Function: which noun or pronoun does it qualify?

Exercise 8
Each of these phrases contains an adjective. State what **kind** it is.

a green pencil, his towel, French scent, some money, twelve runs, this chair, what book? every week, the third man, the Greek temple, a perfect circle, a few apples, neither person, his ears, certain boys, whose shirt? my bicycle, a beautiful face, a second chance, sixty years, her father, Buxton water, that teacher, tasty sandwiches, which newspaper, twenty pounds, marvellous playing, your uncle, South African grapes, some people, those houses, violent moods, a few mistakes, our dog, a terrible accident, half an inch, either dress, a cuddly bear, a white envelope, a Granada programme.

Comment
Define 'a' and 'the' once, and then ignore their reappearances.

'South African' – one part of speech.
'half an inch' – Originally this probably was 'a half of an inch' and in this usage it must be regarded as a **noun**.

Exercise 9
State what **kinds** of adjectives are used here and which **degree** of comparison they are in.

my best friend, the coloured pencil, an older brother, a more intelligent pupil, an interesting book, the finest coffee, a most beautiful sunset, ancient buildings, a blacker cloud, simple arithmetic, the quietest mouse, a more suitable dress, golden wheat, scented flowers, a happier child, that most terrible storm, a much more satisfactory report, a clear mistake, the longest bridge, two further questions.

Comment
'further' – **comparative** degree.

It is interesting to see how the close relationship between noun and adjective has led to the formation of new words. In the animal kingdom we find

greyhound, bluebottle,
redbreast, blackbird,
greenshank, whitethroat

and elsewhere
    quicksilver, deadline,
    longboat, mainland,
    highbrow

and even Shakespeare's 'truepenny' playing witness to this interdependence of the two parts of speech.

Exercises on nouns, pronouns and adjectives taken together
Give A. the kind, number and gender of the nouns,
        B. the kind, gender, number and person of the pronouns and
        C. the kind, degree of comparison and function of the adjectives (what noun or pronoun do they qualify) in these exercises.

Exercise 10
    I told him that the Albert Hall was my favourite building.
    Did that girl have German measles?
    We saw several bees that could not find their swarm.
    For myself, I did not think that the man who was ill was speaking the truth to the doctor.
    I counted eight Canadians in front of us.
    Those plums are sweet but none of these is.
    Has he enough courage to fight the champion, Bruno?
    Who is Lord Lickem? I thought he was an ice-cream salesman.
    See you take some care in that old car.
    That is the nicest thing that woman has said to me this month.

Comment
Watch the word 'that'.

1. In 'I told him that . . .' it is a **conjunction**, linking two parts of the sentence. Ignore it in this sentence.
2. In 'Did that girl . . .' it is an **adjective**, qualifying 'girl'.
3. 'We saw several bees that . . .' it is a **relative pronoun** referring back to 'bees'.
4. 'ill' – This is an **adjective**, qualifying 'who'.

Exercise 11

Parents like children who are well behaved.

You are a better man than I am, if you face him in the boxing-ring.

Those boys can leave early if they like.

It gives me the greatest of pleasure to talk to Henry.

I counted a queue of six buses in the High Street.

Your face looks shinier than his; what about mine?

Every ounce of my strength has been spent putting up that fence.

His good health came from the most strenuous exercise.

'A penny for your thoughts', the Russian dancer said to us.

Give your sisters everything that you have taken from their room.

Verbs: I

It is perhaps no coincidence that verb, vital, versatile and villain begin with the same letter. The alliteration is a clue to the dangers ahead. Certainly, the verb is 'vital'. With its subject noun it anchors the structure of a sentence to a logical mooring-post and virtually orders the other words in a sentence how to group themselves. Its 'versatility' is breath-taking; it can twist its form into different shapes and provide nuances of meaning that reflect the keenest subtleties of a writer's thoughts. But 'villain' it remains; for, unless we get the verb 'right', we can find ourselves without grammatical benchmarks to guide us.

Crucial to our understanding of verb functions are the notions of finiteness and non-finiteness. When the same verb-form can serve both these masters, as it can, only a scrupulous observance of their action can help us. Therefore this distinction is emphasised at the start of this section (see Exercise 12).

The second concern is the heavy armoury of technical terms the verb carries around: no fewer than twenty-four defining terms are used to identify the functions of a verb in a sentence. One might ask: is it necessary to go to these lengths? The answer is 'Yes'. There can be no mastery of the mystery without hard work, yet the pursuit is not without excitement. The intellectual challenge is stimulating, and a clue might be to treat these exercises not so much as chores but more as topics of discussion, referring back to the primer for guidance and example as the occasion arises.

FINITE AND NON-FINITE VERBS

A **finite** verb is limited by a person (who does the action) and the time (when the action is done). A **non-finite** verb has no such limitations placed upon it. E.g.

Tom *told* me *to go* home.

'Told' is a finite verb, limited by Tom (the person) and the past tense (when the action was done).

'To go' has no such limitation – no one 'to go', no time sense in 'to go', so it is non-finite.

The general rule is that when a verb has a 'subject', it is finite.

Exercise 12
The verbs in these sentences are in italics. Some are **finite**, some **non-finite**. Say which are which.

He *wants to play* cricket.
The famous artist *taught* me how *to paint* faces.
I *shall make* you *walk* to school.
Swimming teaches you self-confidence.
Smoking destroys your health.
Walking over the moors *will give* you an appetite.
The car *started going* into a skid.
The stars *seem to shine* more brightly in the North.
The gunmen *threatened to kill* their hostage.
Drinking coffee *keeps* you awake at night.

Comment
'walk' – 'to walk'. Parse accordingly.
'going' – 'to go'.

Exercise 13
To save money *helps* you *to pay* for things you *want to buy*.

To help the aged *makes* a person *feel* good.
Stringing coloured beads on a wire *helped* little Joan *learn* how *to count*.
Catching fish in the stream *meant* James *had* something for the family *to eat*.
The aeroplane *tried to climb to avoid* a collision.
Sunny Spain *provided* the weather for everyone *to enjoy* life.
The matron *told* the nurse *to watch* the new patient.
To see Mount Everest *gives* one a great thrill.
Speaking French, my uncle *made* the gendarme *understand* him.
Dreaming sometimes *leads* to nightmares.

Comment
'feel'   – 'to feel'.
'understand' – 'to understand'.

TENSES

The tense of a verb is the time-slot into which it is placed. For the moment we are concerned with only three: the **past**, the **present** and the **future**.

In the present, things are happening at this moment, now.
In the past, they happened some time ago.
In the future, they have yet to happen, they will do so at some time ahead.

Exercise 14
Give the **tense** of the verb in these phrases.

my dog swims, I walk to school, the bell rang, cattle chew the cud, I shall run in the marathon, the train arrived late, teacher talks a lot, we eat our breakfast, some men work on Sundays, tomorrow Dad will build the shed, tonight you will come home early, the girls waited for a bus, the sun went down, those flowers like the sunlight, the farmer gathered his harvest, we shall go to the football match, they left early, the Queen visits Canada next week, she left the house, the children sat still.

TRANSITIVE AND INTRANSITIVE VERBS

When the action of a verb is 'passed on' to a person or object in a sentence, we say that verb is used **transitively**.

When no action is 'passed on', it is used **intransitively**.

Thus: 'I killed the man in the black suit' – transitive, because the action of killing is 'passed on' to the 'man'.

'I killed just for the fun of it' – intransitive, because the action of killing is not 'passed on' to any person or thing.

Exercise 15
Say whether the verbs in these sentences are used **transitively** or **intransitively**.

The butcher slaughtered the calf.
I gave my sandwiches to my sister.
The car travelled at fifty m.p.h.
In winter the sun sets early.
Lion-tamers frighten the animals into submission.
Drifts of snow pile up very quickly in a high wind.
I found a new chair in my bedroom last night.
Cricket is a very exciting game to watch.

My savings have mounted up to a considerable sum
   in the bank.
He hit the target right in the middle.

PERSON

In grammar there are three **persons** – 1st, 2nd and
3rd.

The 1st person is 'I' or 'we', the person actually
   speaking or doing.
The 2nd person is 'you' (or 'thou'), the person spoken
   to.
The 3rd person is 'he', 'she', 'it' or 'they', the persons
   or things spoken about or acted on.

Exercise 16
Say whether these verbs are in the **1st**, **2nd** or **3rd**
person.

I went home early.
My grant has not come through yet.
Last night you took my coat.
She tells horrible lies.
The train never arrived.
We saw the boys in the field.
You will be there next week?
I found a penny in the street.
In the sun her hair shone like gold.
We shall not come back.

VOICE

There are two voices in grammar: **active** and **passive**.

When the verb is 'in the **active** voice', the subject of the verb does the action.

When the verb is 'in the **passive** voice', the action of the verb is done to the subject. E.g.

I held the reins. **Held** = active voice
  ('I', the subject, did the holding).
The engine pushed the train into the station. **Pushed** = active voice
  ('engine', the subject, did the pushing).
Robert was held for torture. **Was held** = passive voice
  ('Robert', the subject, had the holding done to him).
The train was pushed into the station by the engine. **Was pushed** = passive voice
  ('the train', the subject, received the pushing).

Exercise 17

Say whether these verbs are in the **active** or **passive** voice.

I read the book. The farmer milked the cows. He was bitten by a snake. He is imprisoned in Sicily. The girls love dancing. The room will be painted white. They sang in the choir. The doctor will come later. My uncle drives a Jaguar. Will they be punished for it? London seems very dirty to me. Worms help the grass grow. The band was playing my tune. Football is played in the winter. Six men were rescued from the ship. Jane helped the woman to bed. The table was laid for tea. The Marx brothers make me laugh. You will be paid £4 an hour.

Comment

'will be painted' = **future passive**.

Exercise 18

Argentina were beaten in the World Cup. Sun-rays burn the skin. I like swimming. The bus was stopped by a policeman. My teacher wears old-fashioned clothes. Lunch was cooked by the new French chef. Swimming in the river will be banned next week. Eight boats sailed for Spain. Potatoes are used to make crisps. The natives shot the tiger. Yesterday my brother gave me a present. The book must be returned by Wednesday. Gurkhas are very fine soldiers. He was made captain. Our milkman dropped a crate of bottles. Birds sometimes sing all night. Climbing fills me with excitement. Shall we be given any reward for all our hard work? Silence reigned. The cat sat on the mat while the dog was locked out in the cold.

STRONG AND WEAK VERBS

Verbs are classified as **strong** or **weak** in accordance with the way in which they form their past tenses. Here are some examples:

Present tense	*Past tense*	*Perfect tense*
I walk	I walked	I have walked (weak)
I pick	I picked	I have picked (weak)
I give	I gave	I have given (strong)
I sing	I sang	I have sung (strong)

Exercise 19
Using three columns, complete these verb forms. The present tense is given in each case.

I push him, he says so, they sleep, we send it, he brings them, you speak well, I shoot her, it costs £2, you drink milk, Mum bakes a cake, the wind blows, I see someone, they run away, he beats a drum, you give money, we throw darts, I swim away, the girl sits down, snow melts, she wears shoes, I choose a book, you write a letter, they sing carols, he wins the game, we know that, she tears the paper, I drive the car, he shakes the bottle, you stick the stamp, they ride a bike.

SINGULAR AND PLURAL VERBS

Verbs take their **number** from their subject. Thus: in 'the man went home', 'went' is singular because 'man' is. In 'the boys went home', 'went' is plural because 'boys' is plural.

Exercise 20
Say whether the verbs in these sentences are **singular** or **plural**.

The boy has a scar. My men will build the wall. It looks like rain. The buses were late. You are very untidy today. Has the cat been out? The sheep grazed in the valley. None of the men went home. London and Paris are capital cities. They play cards every night. The team lost its game. Flowers always blossom in the sun. The bee flew to its hive. They always speak quietly. My pencil needs sharpening. We never spill our drinks. The soldiers marched

down the Strand. Ships dock here every night. Pride
goes before a fall. Flocks of birds flew across the sky.

Comment

'you are'   – can be **singular** or **plural**,
                            according to sense.
'Has the cat been out?' – The verb here is 'to be out'.

Exercises on verbs 21

A. Say whether the verbs in italics are **finite** or **non-finite**.

B. If finite, give the **person, number, tense, voice**
of the verb and say whether it is used **transitively**
or **intransitively**.

1. You *sent* me two books *to read*.
2. The men *are coming* home next Tuesday *to spend*
their leave.
3. *Fighting* pollution *will be* the future task for
mankind.
4. The lions *were killed* by men showing no mercy.
5. I *shut* the door *to keep* the draught out.
6. Tom, Mary and Jim *are going* home *to play*
Scrabble.
7. *To sing* like Alice *means practising* very hard.
8. You *will be caught* if you *try to steal* that car.
9. *Going* to school, I usually *run* very fast.
10. My dog *tried to chase* and *catch* a ball, but sadly
was killed.
11. We *like* ice-cream when the weather *is* hot.
12. *To work* hard and *play* hard *seems to be* a good
motto.
13. The boys *stopped* at the door, *fearing* to go in.
14. We *were shocked to find* that he *had played truant*
from school.
15. The aircraft *will take off* at three o'clock.

16. You *say* you *will be calling* at five *to see* if *I'm coming*.
17. The ladies *were* amazed *to see* themselves in the mirror.
18. *Parking* there *is* dangerous if anyone *wants to turn* the corner.
19. The ships *were attacked* as they *turned* into the Channel.
20. We *shall expect to find* you ready *to turn out* and *play* for the team.

Comment
'practising' – **gerund**, non-finite part of verb.
'catch'   = 'to catch'.
'play'   = 'to play' (twice in the exercise).
'amazed'   – **adjective**, qualifying 'ladies'.

Adverbs

The adverb is the verb's best friend, extending and modifying its meaning in a variety of useful and colourful ways. But the adverb is gregarious and shows its favours quite often to adjectives and other adverbs. It has an extensive wardrobe and can appear in many guises. Sometimes good detective work is needed to identify this part of speech, but it is friendly and helpful and should not give rise to any difficulties in grammar exercises.

<u>Remember</u>

Kind: time, place, manner, number, degree, reason, condition, concession, affirmation, negation

Degree: positive, comparative, superlative

Function: modifies verb, adjective or other adverb

Exercise 22
What **kinds** of adverbs are to be found in these sentences?

He will arrive soon. Will you go home? The cat prowled secretly. They knocked twice. The men were greatly overweight. Tell me if you are coming. Although I like him, I don't trust him. It certainly looks good. Do not touch that switch. I must go now.

When you arrive there, knock loudly. It worked well. The train was driven carelessly. You came in late last night. Teacher sent me there. Cunningly the pickpocket took the wallet. He could not even walk home safely. I wonder whether she will come. Yes, I'll go eventually, but not until he asks properly.

Comment
'greatly' – **degree**.
'even'   – **degree**.
'whether' – **condition**.

Exercise 23
Say what **kinds** of adverbs occur in these sentences and which words they modify.

He spoke slowly. She was blissfully happy. That chap moves too suspiciously for my liking. The picture was badly painted. Once I saw her laughing. It was very wrong. The clouds burst suddenly into rain. Unfortunately the child will never recover. That is not my pen. Africa is a terribly dry continent. I am extremely grateful for your help.

Exercise 24
Say whether any of these adverbs are in the **comparative** or **superlative** degree.

Compact disc sets will be more readily available soon.
She sang most successfully last night.
They were helplessly adrift at sea.
The bullfrog croaked most hideously in the dark.
Fortunately no one had left.
Her luggage was excessively overweight.
The M6 is more easily found than the M5.
The settee is much more awkwardly placed there.

All contributions most gratefully received.
The professor lectured most learnedly last night.

(Note: In some cases, adverbial conjunctions have been regarded as adverbs in these sentences to avoid complications at this stage.)

Apposition

'Apposition' means placed opposite, against. In the sentences that follow, some nouns are mentioned twice; once in general terms and, a second time, by a more particular name. The second noun is said to be in **apposition** to the first and acquires the same grammatical status – number, gender and case – as its forerunner.

Exercise 25
Say which words are in **apposition** to those in italics in these sentences:

My cousin Jim, the pop star, will arrive next week.
Did you see *The Challenger*, the American rocket, land yesterday?
I gave him that new *book* to read, 'How To Murder Your Teacher'.
His *uncle* Bill sent Harry, my friend, a Walkman for his birthday.
The *famous steam-train*, The Flying Scotsman, is now a tourist attraction.
The astronomer showed me the new *star* he had found, the Twinkling Eyeball.
I bought my friend a *drink*, a lemonade, when we went out.
The *rally* on the Isle of Man, the famous T.T. race, always draws a big crowd.
Come over here, *boy*, you with the red tie I mean, John Spinks.

(Note the positions of the commas in these sentences.)

Complements

If a noun or pronoun used with part of the verb 'to be' is followed by another noun, this second noun is said to be a **complement** of the first, and again acquires the grammatical status of its precursor.

Exercise 26
In these sentences, which word is a **complement** to the word in italics?

That *man* is my father.
She is the schoolteacher I told you about.
Copenhagen is the capital city of Denmark.
The last *man* out of the wreck was Tom Smith.
Honesty is the best policy.
'*As You Like It*' is a romantic play by William Shakespeare.
The *boys* over there are visitors from Italy.
The three silver *spoons* will be the last pieces I need for the set.
Soldiers are only civilians dressed up in uniform.
Sultanas are the best fruit for scones.

Prepositions

These small words introduce a phrase, and link verbal and noun ideas in a sentence.

Exercise 27
Identify the **prepositions** in the following phrases:

over the fence, without his shirt, unlike his brother, in bed, above the roof, along the edge, by himself, outside my shop, with a laugh, from six o'clock, to the fair, about eight foot high, in the kitchen, for nothing, into the building, down the bank, on the table, before the war, up the pole, off the chair.

Exercise 28
Write out the prepositional **phrase** which belongs to the preposition in italics.

Give him the book *for* his homework.
From my position the leading runner is the Kenyan.
Go down *to* the docks and see if the ship is in.
I want you to help Susan put little Peter *to* bed.
The ball has gone *over* the fence again.
Mr Brown left the office *without* a word.
By working hard Keith reached a good standard *in* maths.
Leave the letter *on* the desk before you go.
Don't knock the ornament *off* the shelf as you pass.
Nine *into* twenty does not go exactly.

Conjunctions

The **conjunction** is a link that joins two other words
or ideas together.

Exercise 29
Identify the **conjunctions** in these sentences:

She and I are lost.
Tom and Jerry will be hurt.
She said neither you nor I could go.
You may take one but leave some for the others.
Sally can't come with us, neither can you.
I told William that he was lucky to be alive.
The lion did not attack because he was not hungry.
Derek is not as fast at running as you are.
My brother is older than both of us.
I'll call for you after I've done my homework.
Sit still and keep quiet.
Shall I give them fish or meat for supper?
John runs very fast but I can jump much higher than
   he can.
The judge said that the prisoner was not to be
   released.
Sam, Matt and Peggy all bought an ice-cream.
I shall be there as soon as I have washed my hair.
Be home early tonight because father's going out.
The singer was good, but we didn't like her dress.

PART II: INTERMEDIATE EXERCISES

This section is concerned mainly with the use of the verb in more detail. First, the unusual phenomenon of **case** is explained, followed by a set of exercises to consolidate this new knowledge and to point up the dependence of noun/pronoun and verb on each other.

Different aspects of use of the verb are then discussed: tenses, moods, uses of participles and gerunds, auxiliary verbs, which are followed by revision tests for consolidation.

This part of the manual concludes with sections on prepositions, conjunctions and the use of commas and hyphens.

Case

The **case** of a noun or pronoun in English grammar is a statement about the way it relates to another word in that sentence: usually it is to the verb; sometimes to another noun or pronoun or a preposition. There are some technical uses of words here that need to be understood.

Subject: This is the person or thing that is the doer, the actor, in the sentence, the one we are writing about.

The *king* went aboard his ship.
The *ball* was kicked into the net.

Object: This is the person or thing at whom or to whom the action is directed.

The army promoted *Sir John* to the rank of major.
She swept the *floor* twice a day.

From these two words have come 'subjective' and 'objective' cases. To keep in line with usage in other languages, however, we shall employ the terms **nominative** (for subject) and **accusative** (for object).

There is a third case: **possessive**. As the word indicates, this case arises when a noun possesses something:

My *father's* car is in the garage.
The *gate's* lock had fallen off.
The *girls'* umbrellas were stolen.

(Note the different position of the apostrophe when the words are singular and plural.)

In this book we shall use the word **genitive** for the possessive case.

Note: In other languages (Latin, German), we meet another term, the **dative** case, but this term is generally disregarded in English. It applies to indirect objects which, in English, are governed by the preposition 'to'.

Exercises on case

Remember

There are three cases: nominative
                               accusative
                               genitive

Only nouns and pronouns have a **case**.

1. The **nominative** case is used when the word is the **subject** of a verb.

2. The **accusative** case is used (a) when the word is a **direct object** or an **indirect object** after a verb; (b) when the word is governed by a **preposition**.

3. The **genitive** case is used when the word shows **possession**.

Words in **apposition**, or used as **complements**, and **gerunds** and **participles** also have a **case** according to the way they are used.

Case applies to all nouns and pronouns whenever they occur.

Exercise 30

State which nouns and pronouns are in the **nominative** case in these sentences and indicate the verbs of which they are the subjects:

My son works at I.C.I. They went home early. For three months the workmen were on strike. Henry Ford made the first people's car. We sing hymns each day. Tomorrow they are having a party. Without saying a word, my father went to bed. I woke up at four o'clock. John and Kitty looked very smart. Maisie is getting married on Sunday and we shall be there.

Comment

Nominatives: son, they, workmen, Henry Ford, we, they, father, I, John/Kitty, Maisie, we.

Exercise 31

He talks all the time. The daughter of the man next door threw my ball back to me. Without stopping to think, the doctor injected the patient. You can't bring the dog in here! The goal-scorer, running back to the line, smiled up at the fans. Suddenly she ran into the street. Last night, at about ten o'clock, the burglar-alarm went off. In front of the class, the teacher asked me to stand up. It takes a lot of courage to use a parachute. The train came in very late.

Comment

Nominatives: He, daughter, doctor, you, goal-scorer, she, burglar-alarm, teacher, it, train.

Exercise 32

The nouns and pronouns in italics in these sentences are subjects of verbs, or are complements or in apposition to other words. All are in the **nominative** case. Say which they are, and what verbs or other words they relate to:

My *mother*, now *Mrs Mary Williams*, told me all about herself.

They are my *brothers* over there.

At the seaside, *Danny* met two of his friends.

Tom and *Mary*, my first *cousins*, called for me to go to the concert.

Jogging every morning is a very healthy *exercise*.

Outside the Town Hall, the *cars* were moving very slowly.

It must be the *milkman* at the door.

That history *book* is a favourite *one* of my father's.

We shot down three aircraft in that battle.

Blackpool, the most popular seaside *town* in Britain, attracts thousands of visitors every year.

Exercise 33

Copper is a most precious *metal*.

Over by the dresser *I* have put your present.

That *Tibbles*, the *menace*, is the naughtiest *kitten* in the world!

You worked well last night, *John*.

Tom's *brother*, *Clive*, is the fastest *swimmer* in the school.

They don't seem to worry about anything.

Music is the only *thing* in the world for me.

Without seeing it first, *he* bought a car for £200.

The *Daily Scream* was the first *newspaper* to print the story.

The *film*, 'Lost Horizon', was a *masterpiece*.

Exercise 34

In these sentences, some nouns are in the **accusative** case because they are either direct or indirect objects of a verb. Say which they are, and give the verbs that govern them.

The headmaster sent John home.
Yesterday I saw two men fighting in the street.
My cousin gave me a £1 coin.
The company sent Philip the record-album yesterday.
The fierce wave smashed the sea-wall to pieces.
My Granny gives my sister and me our tea every night.
Poor health forced the shop assistant to retire.
The chemical company found Mr Walker a new job last week.
You ought to give him another chance.
Poverty teaches us new ways of making ends meet.

Comment

Accusatives: John, men, me (ind.), coin, record-album, Philip (ind.), sea-wall, tea, me (ind.), sister (ind.), assistant, job, Mr Walker (ind.) chance, him (ind.), ways, us (ind.).

Exercise 35

The pensioner claimed another £5 for his wife.
While I waited, the clerk stamped my passport.
Shall I send Mary a card for her birthday?
Without hesitating, the prisoner opened the door and escaped.
After that attack he will revenge himself.
Last Friday I gave Jim my best pen.
The battleship flashed a signal to the rest of the fleet.

The ambulance brigade provide an excellent service for the sick.

Fourteen cups of tea he drank without pausing in between.

Didn't the teacher give the class a good telling off today?

Comment

Accusatives: £5, passport, card, Mary (ind.), door, himself, pen, Jim (ind.), signal, service, cups, telling off, class (ind.).

Exercise 36

These sentences contain examples of nouns or pronouns in the **accusative** case which are governed by prepositions. Which are they, and which prepositions govern them?

Outside the station the bus stopped for an hour.

I spoke to him about his manners.

The strength of his character was obvious to all of us.

People in the USA seem to like a lot of noise and bustle.

Without my help, she pushed the car into the garage for me.

After the match the team thanked the Vicar for his help.

In the office the staff were working in silence.

The comet went across the sky in a blaze of white light.

He stood against the wall in front of the umpire.

The tigress played with her cubs among the trees on the edge of the jungle.

Note: There are 27 instances of the accusative case.

Exercise 37

Here are examples of nouns or pronouns in the **accusative** case which are governed by non-finite forms of the verb; e.g. the infinitive, participle or verbal noun.

He tried to *hit* me ('me' object of 'to hit')
Tossing the *ball* into the air ('ball' object of 'tossing')
I do not like *peeling* onions ('peeling' object of 'like')

Which are they, and what words govern them in the following sentences?

The clock began to strike the hour.
Calling him in for tea, Mother set the table.
They love teasing poor Kitty.
Sinking the 'Bismarck' was not an easy task.
Industry, demanding more production, has begun reshaping itself.
It was impossible to see the monkeys up the tree.
Would you like to tell me what you are doing?
Selling lampshades in the market, he made a small fortune.
The French are clever at designing clothes for women.
The Russian champion managed to hurl the javelin further than anyone else.

Comment
    'the hour' gov. by 'to strike'
    'him' gov. by 'calling'
    'Kitty' gov. by 'teasing'
    'Bismarck' gov. by 'sinking'
    'production' gov. by 'demanding'
    'monkeys' gov. by 'to see'
    'me' gov. by 'to tell'

'lampshades' gov. by 'selling'
'clothes' gov. by 'designing'
'javelin' gov. by 'to hurl'

Exercise 38

To run a mile in four minutes was Alec's ambition.
She loved cooking pasta dishes for her family.
Singing hymns in the bath, Bill was not very popular
   with the neighbours.
The ship came into the harbour to unload her cargo.
Not to take any notice of your teacher is very foolish.
A black cloud passed over, creating a dark shadow
   over the land.
Joining the army at seventeen was Max's great
   ambition.
The judge told the prisoner that sentencing him to
   serve five years was very lenient.
To save the population from starving, Mary volun-
   teered to raise more money for food.
Crooning love-songs into the microphone, the pop
   star looked as if he was about to cry.

Exercise 39

In these sentences are nouns and pronouns showing
possession, which are in the **genitive** case. Say which
they are.

John's pencil-box was missing today.
The car's doors had been scratched by vandals.
I suppose the cat's dish is empty again.
That saucepan is not mine. Is it yours?
The Italian was stranded in the midst of London's
   traffic.
In our house the week's best meal is Sunday lunch.
Did you do Mrs Jackson's shopping for her today?
The noise of a rifle shot shattered the village's
   silence.

The Smith's curtains look as though they could do with a wash.

The film's attraction was the powerful way in which the actors played their parts.

Note: 'Is it yours?' 'yours' is genitive.

Verbs: II

TENSES

Exercises in tenses are divided as follows:

In the **active** voice: past, perfect and pluperfect
present, future and future perfect
conditional

In the **passive** voice: past, perfect and pluperfect
present, future and future perfect
conditional

State the tense of the verb in each sentence.

Exercise 40 Active voice, past, perfect and pluperfect tenses

The sailor gave his hammock to his friend.

Last week her husband tried to build a wall.

That was before the workman had laid a new water-main.

Sarah has baked a lovely chicken pie.

The old man went into a home for the aged.

General Salutem inspected the 3rd Company of the regiment.

Molly has worked with that firm for ten years.

We had known about the missing money for months.

Mr and Mrs Perkins have booked a holiday in Spain.

Jim and Mary sang in the church choir.

Exercise 41 *Passive voice, perfect and pluperfect tenses*

Charlie Johnson was killed during an armed robbery.

Sadly my cousin has been charged with speeding.

The terrorists had been questioned about the bomb.

My sister was given a beautiful present by her fiancé.

The ambassador has been received by the Queen.

I had been rowing for three hours and was exhausted.

The two prisoners have been taken to Colchester.

The main streets were swept clean last night.

By two o'clock I was being prepared for the operation.

The aircraft had been grounded because of an accident.

Exercise 42 *Active voice, present, future and future perfect tenses*

Your homework is terribly untidy.

The flight will have left before you reach the airport.

Tomorrow the team will play in the final.

This afternoon the gardener hopes to have time to cut the grass.

We will share our good fortune with all the family.

Next week the exam will take place on Tuesday morning.

It lasts ten minutes and then fizzles out.

All the soup will have disappeared before you sit down.

The cricket match looks like a fiasco in this rain.

I shall have washed and dressed before you are out of bed.

Exercise 43 Passive voice, present, future and future perfect tenses

You will be punished for your disgraceful behaviour.

I am shocked to hear about your bad fortune.

By next February those trees will have been planted in our garden for twenty years.

The carpet is cleaned at least twice a week.

I shall be examined by the doctor tomorrow.

He is charged with shoplifting.

You don't know if you will be accepted until next week.

That naughty child is being told off by his mother.

The fruit will have been inspected by the health official before they sell it.

Note: The exercises which follow give examples of the verb used in a continuous sense, where the action is spread over a period of time. Here again, can you identify the appropriate verb forms?

Exercise 44 Active voice, past, perfect and pluperfect continuous tenses

When the bell went, the master had been telling the class about Napoleon.

The passengers were sitting on the deck in the sun.

For three weeks I have been trying to repair this dishwasher.

We were walking by the Town Hall when the storm broke.

The crisis in the docks had been coming for a long time.

The idea of flying has been worrying my Grannie for weeks.

They were drinking whisky by the time I arrived.

Those shoes have been pinching your toes ever since you bought them.

Louise has been spending too much money on cosmetics.

The James family were staying in the South of France this summer.

Exercise 45 *Active voice, present, future and future perfect continuous tenses*

Aunt Polly is nagging Uncle Alf again.

The Commanding Officer will be inspecting camp tomorrow.

By tonight I shall have been waiting three days for him to arrive.

Will they be wanting coffee after dinner, ma'am?

The taxis are waiting for the ten-thirty train to arrive.

If it doesn't stop by tomorrow, it will have been raining for five days without a break.

You are talking a lot of nonsense.

He will be coming home late after the party.

They will have stayed at the hotel three days longer than they anticipated.

John will be riding in the park early in the morning.

The boss told his staff that they would be informed about the vacancies later.

The trains should be running on time by next week.

I should sell my car, if I were you; the time is ripe.

His wife wanted to know if he would be ready to go by six.

You know, we should have thought about that before.

If the weather was fine, he thought the charity race would raise about £1,000 for the hospital.

Exercise 46 *Passive voice, conditional and past conditional tenses*

The book would have been sold if he had reduced the price.

That chair should have been chopped up for firewood.

The President would have been assassinated if his guards had not saved him.

The letter should be posted before the next collection.

The bus should be serviced before it goes out again.

I would have been baffled if anyone asked me that question.

By tomorrow the team for the weekend should have been picked.

We should never have been attacked if our position had not been so exposed.

The Johnsons would be sent to prison if they did not have such a good lawyer.

My dad says he would have been shot if he had turned in a piece of homework like that.

MOODS

The 'mood' of a verb is the form it takes to express a particular manner of conveying meaning. Thus, a command uses the **imperative** mood, a wish or supposition the **subjunctive** mood, an expression not limited in time the **infinitive** mood, and everyday expressions the **indicative** mood. This section will discuss the first three of these moods.

Remember

There are four moods: indicative
                              imperative
                              subjunctive
                              infinitive

The imperative mood

Exercise 47
Identify the **imperative** forms in these sentences:

Come in, Tom.

Write to me soon.

Stand still, everyone.

Do your shoelaces up.

Cross the road now.

Try the other shoe.

Fix the light for me.

Have another piece of cake.

Put your hands up.

Take me home, please.

Do not come near me.

Do not write your name in ink.

Don't stand on that carpet.

Don't do that now.

Don't cross that bridge.

Don't try to be funny.

Don't fix it like that.

Don't have too much to drink.

Don't put your foot on the brake.

Don't take it too badly.

Comment
In negative forms, the actual verb is 'do come' 'do write' 'do stand', etc.

The subjunctive mood

Exercise 48
Identify the **subjunctive** forms in these conditional clauses:

If I were the Prime Minister, I would declare war on drugs.

If she were a famous ballerina, she wouldn't be driving an old Beetle.

If Dick were here now, he would soon sort you out.

If we were Martians, we would arrange for space flights back to Mars.

If Sheila were Cleopatra, I'd audition for the part of Mark Antony.

The infinitive mood can take the following forms:

present infinitive	(active)	to take
	(passive)	to be taken
perfect infinitive	(active)	to have taken
	(passive)	to have been taken
present continuous infinitive		to be taking
perfect continuous infinitive		to have been taking

Note: The infinitive form is normally preceded by 'to', but this may be omitted.

Exercise 49 Present and present continuous forms, active and passive
Identify the **infinitives** in these sentences and say what kind they are:

She said she did not want to be selling dresses all her life.

To be held in prison without charge is illegal in this country.

Mary left the party early to catch the last bus home.

The gangsters tried to make him reveal the secret code.

Do you have to be asking questions all the time?

To be paid more than Bill, you will have to work much harder.

The Captain wanted to see his sailors load the guns for action.

The young man noticed the car follow him down the road.

The opera has to be sung in English, I'm afraid.
He did not want to be seen in the pub.

Comment

'to be selling'	– pres. continuous active
'To be held'	– pres. passive
'to catch'	– pres. active
'to make'	– pres. active
'reveal' (= 'to reveal')	– pres. active
'to be asking'	– pres. continuous active
'to be paid'	– pres. passive
'to work'	– pres. active
'to see'	– pres. active
'load' (= 'to load')	– pres. active
'follow' (= 'to follow')	– pres. active
'to be sung'	– pres. passive
'to be seen'	– pres. passive

Exercise 50 Perfect form, active and passive

The waitress was supposed to have laid the table an
hour ago.

The author said he seemed to have been working on
the book for over a year, but it still was not ready.

That bill was due to have been paid a week ago.

To have sailed across the Atlantic single-handed
was Pamela's great ambition.

The treasure was reported to have been buried on a
remote island in the Indian Ocean.

The defendant was known to have been lying about
the robbery from the beginning.

To have shot down twenty-five enemy aircraft was
S/Ldr Janson's claim to fame.

The young lady was delighted to have been asked to
go to the party.

John seemed to have been catching buses all his life.

To have been painted by Arturo Gattoni was a great
privilege for the Princess.

Comment

'to have laid'	– perfect active
'to have been working'	– perfect cont. active
'to have been paid'	– perfect passive
'to have sailed'	– perfect active
'to have been buried'	– perfect passive
'to have been lying'	– perfect cont. active
'to have shot down'	– perfect active
'to have been asked'	– perfect passive
'to have been catching'	– perfect cont. active
'to have been painted'	– perfect passive

Exercise 51 (see also p. 161, and Exercise 121)
Rewrite these sentences avoiding the **split infinitives**:

I told him to never talk like that again.

The man sent me to quickly bring him a paper.

To suddenly jump on to a moving van can be dangerous.

Mum asked him not to so noisily eat his food.

The sailor had to carefully steer through the narrow channel.

To never see her brother again was too much for Mary.

He wanted to urgently reach home before dark.

Liverpool seems to always be in the news.

To simply say you won't come is not good enough.

My pigeon is able to equally well race against any in the club.

PARTICIPLES

Participles end in -ing or -ed, though strong verbs have other forms. The -ing form is the **present participle**, the -ed form the **past participle**. They are used as **adjectives**, but can have objects of their own. E.g.

The duplicating machine. The battered old hat.
Turning the corner, the car suddenly stopped.
Caught in a trap, the thief gave up.
With an object:
Finding a sixpence, Jenny ran home.
Hiding his torn jacket in the cupboard, John pretended nothing had happened.

Exercise 52

Identify the **participles** in these sentences. Say what kind they are, what their function is and if they have an object.

Walking in the park, he saw his brother approaching.

Mrs Smith found some peace, switching off the television.

The porter was happy, looking forward to retirement.

Having planted his potatoes, my friend set about putting in some beans and carrots.

Rescued from the sea, the survivors turned to thank the brave lifeboatmen.

Singing a solo at the concert, Betty's daughter was a real success.

My uncle passes his days collecting old pebbles from the beach.

Having been defeated in the last match, the other team agreed to concede.

Warned about his lateness, the worker decided to buy an alarm clock.

Being made redundant, Peter was forced to go in for a retraining programme.

Comment

'walking'   – pres. active, adjective

'approaching'	– pres. active, adjective
'switching off'	– pres. active, adj., 'television'
'looking forward'	– present active, adjective
'having planted'	– perfect active, adjective, 'potatoes'
'putting in'	– not a participle, but a gerund
'rescued'	– past active, adjective
'singing'	– pres. active, adj. 'solo'
'collecting'	– not a participle, but a gerund
'having been defeated'	– perfect passive, adj.
'warned'	– past active, adj.
'being made redundant'	– pres. passive, adjective. The argument here is that the verb is 'to make redundant', not simply 'to make'.

GERUNDS

Gerunds also are parts of a verb that end in -ing, but they have more of an independent life than participles. They are **nouns**, names of actions, and they, too, can have objects of their own.

Exercise 53
Identify the **gerunds** in these sentences and say if they have objects of their own. Give the case the gerund is in.

Carrying coal in those heavy sacks can strain a man's back.
The teacher accused him of deliberately forgetting to bring his homework to school.

His parents did not like to see Roger's chasing around on his motor-cycle.

The dog's barking drove us all silly.

The guard stopped the express by signalling with his lamp.

The priest thought the woman's whistling in church was most inappropriate.

Mending and ironing seemed to occupy my old aunt every night of the week.

The woman could not pass the hall without thinking of her daughter's wedding.

I thought I heard crying coming from the back bedroom.

Stealing the clock from the police station was a source of pride for the crook.

Before dressing yourself, you would do well to wash your face, young man.

I did not approve of the Emperor's handling of the uprising in the eastern province.

Comment

'carrying'	– subj. nom., 'coal', present
'forgetting'	– acc. ('of'), 'to bring', present
'chasing'	– acc., present
'barking'	– nom., present
'signalling'	– acc. ('by'), present
'whistling'	– nom., present
'mending' and 'ironing'	– nom., present
'thinking'	– acc. ('without'), present
'crying'	– acc., present
'stealing'	– nom., present, 'clock'
'dressing'	– acc. ('before'), present, 'yourself'
'handling'	– acc., objective of 'approve of', present
'uprising'	– acc. ('of'), present

AUXILIARY VERBS

These are used with ordinary verbs to give added nuances of meaning. They should be treated as if they were part of the main verb, as one entity. It is useful to note that the 'main' verb is frequently the infinitive form without the word 'to' in front. They do have a meaning of their own and can be used as principal verbs in their own right.

<u>Remember</u>

The auxiliary verbs are: to be

          can

          ought

          do

          to have

          may

          used to

Exercise 54
Parse the verbs in italics in these sentences.

Did you say I *could come* late to school tomorrow?

The soldiers *might be separated* when the battle starts.

May I look at your book for a moment?

The cows *ought to be milked* before tea, Tom.

Those people *could not have come* at a more awkward time.

Bob *used to be* my best friend.

Your sister *may have been delayed* by the weather.

The authority *can be prosecuted* for leaving the road in that state.

Those cups *ought* not *to have been filled* so full.
Used your grandmother *to send* you some money on
your birthday?

Comment

'could come'
— from verb 'to come',
conjugated with aux.
'could', intransitive,
active, 1st pers. sing.,
pres. indicative

'might be separated'
— from verb 'to separate',
conjugated with aux.
'might', intrans., passive,
3rd pers. plural, pres.
indicative

'may look'
— from verb 'to look' conjugated with aux. 'may',
intrans., active, 1st pers.
sing., pres. indicative

'ought to be milked'
— from verb 'to milk' conjugated with aux. 'ought',
intrans., passive, 3rd
pers. plural, present
indicative

'could have come'
— from verb 'to come' conjugated with aux. 'could',
intrans., active, 3rd pers.
plural, perfect indicative

'used to be'
— from verb 'to be', conjugated with aux. 'used',
intrans., active, 3rd pers.
sing., past indicative

'may have been delayed'
— from verb 'to delay', conjugated with aux. 'may',
intrans., passive, 3rd
pers. sing., perfect
indicative

'can be prosecuted'	– from verb 'to prosecute', conjugated with aux. 'can', intrans., passive, 3rd pers. sing., present indicative
'ought to have been filled'–	from verb 'to fill', conjugated with aux. 'ought to', intrans., passive, 3rd pers. plural, perfect indicative
'used to send'	– from verb 'to send', conjugated with aux. 'used to', transitive, active, 3rd pers. singular, past indicative

Questions and negatives with verbs

Compound verbs, which are formed when questions are asked or negative statements are made, need to be identified with care. E.g.

In the sentence: 'You can't go home yet', the actual verb is 'can go'; 'not' has intervened to negate the sense of the meaning but is not part of the verb.
Similarly: In 'Are you still looking for the book?' the verb is 'are looking'; the inversion occurs because of the question, and other words have separated the two parts of the verb.

Exercise 55
Identify the **verbal component** in these sentences.

The choir had not been recently attending rehearsals at the Philharmonic Hall.
Does that handsome cousin of yours come here very often?

Have you really seriously been looking for a new car?

I should certainly never have been setting out for London so late in the day.

Did the American Air Force last year actually launch a rocket to Venus?

The sausages cannot be properly cooked before one o'clock.

Can your friend Rory, the one with the red hair, regularly jog for two hours every night?

Shall we ever, do you think, see a sunset as lovely as that one we saw last night?

Peggy would certainly not happily have gone shopping with her mother.

Those boys could very likely be handsomely rewarded for rescuing that child from drowning.

Comment

had been attending, does come, have been looking, should have been setting out, did launch, can be cooked, can jog, shall see, do think, would have gone, could be rewarded.

Abbreviated forms of 'to be' and 'to have'

It is well to be aware of the abbreviated forms of these two auxiliaries.

am	– I'm
is	– he's, she's, it's, that's, there's
are	– you're, we're, they're
has	– he's, she's, it's, that's, there's
shall/will	– I'll, he'll, she'll, we'll, you'll, they'll
have	– I've, you've, we've, they've
had	– I'd, you'd, he'd, she'd, we'd, they'd

Also note: won't, can't, don't, isn't, aren't; shan't and
          ain't are both colloquial.

When parsing, extend these abbreviations fully:

   I'm going = I am going
   he's home = he is home
   she's arrived = she has arrived
   they'll sing = they will sing
   it's been raining = it has been raining
   it's early = it is early

General revision exercises on verbs
Examples of parsing verbs:

'We **were sitting** in the kitchen'
'were sitting'   – Finite verb, transitive, active voice, 1st person plural, past continuous tense, of 'to sit', indicative mood.

'For **driving** a car while drunk he **was fined** £200'
'driving'   – Non-finite gerund, used as a noun, accusative case governed by preposition 'for', with object 'car'.
'was fined'   – Finite verb, intransitive, passive, 3rd person singular, past tense of 'to fine', indicative mood.

'The ship **had** not **been** completely **wrecked** in the storm'
'had been wrecked' – Finite verb, intransitive, passive, 3rd person singular, pluperfect tense of verb 'to wreck', indicative mood.

Exercise 56
Parse the verbs in italics:

Palm trees *provide* shade in tropical islands.
Send that horrid boy to me.
After *cycling* ten miles, John *breezed* into the house,
  smiling.
If the dustman *had been thinking to give* us a miss, he
  would have had to face me the next day.
The birthday party *will cost* £100, without *counting*
  the cake.
Don't think for one moment that you *will be rewarded*
  for *catching* the thief.
Sounding her siren, the great ship *is sailing* into port.
France *has been celebrating* its 1789 revolution and
  will obviously *continue to do* so for some time.
If the weather *were* not so cold, the children *said* they
  would have gone skating today.

Comment

'provide'	– present tense
'send'	– imperative
'smiling'	– pres. part., qualifying 'John'
'had been thinking'	– pluperfect cont. tense
'to give'	– infinitive, obj. of 'had been thinking'
'would have had'	– past conditional tense
'to face'	– obj. of 'would have had'
'sounding'	– pres. part., qualifying 'ship'
'will continue'	– is the verb
'were'	– subjunctive
'skating'	– pres. part., qualifying 'they'

Exercise 57
  Take that towel and *stop* the fight.
  Has the elephant in Africa really *become* extinct
  because of *hunting?*

Despite the fact that the moon *has been conquered* by man, Mrs Brown still *could* not *find* a plumber *to mend* her cistern.

They *tell* me that I *might*, if I *am* careful, *save* £100.

Digging up corpses *to sell* to doctors *to practise* on *was* the man's way of *earning* a living.

The factory *will be closed* unless someone *agrees to find* some more money.

He *was reported to have been killed* in the accident.

The scientist *says* he *knows* that they *have been adding* chemicals to the food.

Will you please *try to keep* in the queue for *collecting* your wages?

I *should have* certainly *been told* about the *missing* man.

Comment

'take', 'stop'	– imperatives
'has . . . become'	– is the verb
'to mend'	– infinitive used as adj. qualifying 'plumber'
'might . . . save'	– is the verb
'digging'	– gerund, subj. of 'was'
'to sell'	– infinitive used adverbially with 'digging'
'to practise'	– what kinds of 'corpses'? Ones 'to practise on' = infinitive used as adj.
'to have been killed'	– perfect passive infinitive, used as adj. to qualify 'he'
'should have been told'	– is the verb

Prepositions and Conjunctions

Exercise 58
Identify the **prepositions** in these sentences and state
which noun or pronoun they govern:

Come inside the flight-deck and have a look at the
   instruments.
The referee took the ball with him into the changing-
   room.
Without looking, the driver turned the corner, and
   in a flash the cyclist was knocked off his bike.
I've paid for it, and without any further fuss I want
   you to send it to Mother as a present.
In spite of the rain, we said we'd go to the fair with
   them, at least for half an hour.
Apples with cheese and bananas with cream, those
   are my favourites.
She announced that the train standing at Platform
   5 would leave in five minutes for Bristol.
I have nothing against him, but he's always at the
   door of his house watching us.
Are you playing cards with us tonight at the whist
   drive?
On Friday, at six o'clock, they'll separate the green
   boxes from the red ones.

Comment
   inside, at, with, into, without, in, off, for, without,
   to, as, In, of, to, with, at ('least' = noun), for, with,
   with, at, in, for, against, at, of, with, at, On, at,
   from.

Exercise 59

Identify the **conjunctions** in these sentences and say whether they are subordinating or co-ordinating:

The officer told his men that they would attack soon.
Either we go in the car or we don't go at all.
Mother liked her new hat but was too shy to wear it.
The door was locked, so they had to climb through the window.
The sun will never shine unless the wind blows the clouds away.
Can you tell me if the last bus has gone?
That the wall is leaning to the left is obvious to anyone.
One or the other will do for Tommy.
The iron ring is missing, therefore the machine will not function properly.
You and Jimmy get dressed at once or you will go without your breakfast.

Comment

that (sub.), Either (co.), or (co.), but (sub.), so (sub.), unless (sub.), if (sub.), That (sub.), or (co.), therefore (sub.), and (co.), or (co.).

Commas

Exercise 60
Insert commas where they are needed. Do not put them in unnecessarily.

The minister told his congregation what time the services would be held.

Chief Tarabom known everywhere for his fearless courage celebrates twenty years of rule today.

The Frenchman who sat down in the corner looked very suspicious to me.

That woman who was wearing a yellow coat came into my shop last night.

When Alice visits her sister she usually takes her some chocolates.

The chef ordered the waiter whether he liked it or not to wash the dishes.

Lord Clive suggested that his chauffeur should change his uniform as it was dirty.

The fence that runs between our two gardens needs repairing.

The Eiffel Tower that stands in the centre of Paris must be one of the wonders of the modern world.

John says he can't save any money even though he's earning more now than ever before.

Comment
'The Minister . . .'   – no commas
'Chief Tarabom, known . . . courage, celebrates . . .'
'The Frenchman . . .' – no commas
'That woman . . .'   – no commas
'When Alice . . .'   – no commas

'The chef ordered the waiter, whether . . . not, to
wash . . .'
'Lord Clive . . .'   – no commas
'The fence . . .'   – no commas
'The Eiffel Tower, that . . . Paris, must be . . .'
'John says he can't save any money, even . . .'
(optional)

Hyphens

'Well' is joined by a hyphen to an adjective when the phrase is used attributively (in numbers 1, 3, 5), but not when the use is predicative (numbers 2, 4, 6).

1. Shakespeare is a well-known playwright.
2. Shakespeare's plays are well known.
3. The well-known branch of 'Sell-it-All' was crowded today.
4. Harrods shop is well known.
5. He owned a well-established factory in London.
6. After two years the business was well established.

Exercise 61
Insert a hyphen where it is needed in these sentences:

Flying Filly looks a well bred horse to me.

Mary saw that dust had collected on her dressing table.

We'll stop at the half way house on our journey to see the Flying Saucer.

Put the cloves in the spice box on the top shelf.

The firm gave him a company car as part of the good will of the job.

That looks like a well constructed piece of equipment he is using.

Gregorovitch is a foreign sounding name, if you ask me.

Use your dictionary, not guess work, to verify your spellings.

The pilot had a bird's eye view of the whole of south east England.

Comment

well-bred, dressing-table, half-way, spice-box, good-will, well-constructed, foreign-sounding, guesswork, bird's-eye, south-east.

General revision exercises
Parse all words.

Exercise 62

The medical profession had been warned about the danger of Asian flu.

The experts themselves will soon come to see how faster cars can lead to more deaths on the road.

First at the post today, that young Cuban athlete should be watched very carefully in the future.

Mothers and daughters were the most regular attenders at the six sessions we arranged.

A newspaper editor has been described as a man who knows precisely what he wants, but isn't quite sure.

Switch that light off before it gives us away.

One must never go where one has not been invited.

John Wesley, the eighteenth-century Methodist preacher, wrote hundreds of very fine hymns that we still sing in our churches.

My father always said that it is better to come at the latter end of a feast than at the beginning of a fight.

At the foot of the Egyptian pyramids, Napoleon was reported as saying to his soldiers that forty centuries looked down on them.

Comment

'First'	– adj. qualifying 'athlete'
'what he wants'	– 'what' = 'that which', and is a relative pronoun, acc. case after

	verb 'wants'. Its antecedent is understood – 'that', or 'that thing', 'that service'
'it gives us away'	– verb = 'to give away'
'where'	– relative pronoun, 'to that place which . . .' 'Where' is a very versatile word. The sentence could be written: 'One must never go to that place to which . . .' Thus 'where' acts adverbially towards verb 'to go' and as an object of verb/preposition 'to invite to'. Parse: rel. pronoun used adverbially with verb 'to invite', with antecedent (understood) 'that place'
'(hymns) that'	– rel. pronoun
'(always said) that'	– conjunction
'to come'	– in apposition to 'it'
'(soldiers) that'	– conjunction

Exercise 63

He who wants to enter Paradise must have a good key.

On the stage a troupe of dancers has been rehearsing since ten o'clock this morning.

That judge showed no mercy to the gang of robbers who were found guilty of murder.

Choose those if you wish; I think they are left-overs from the jumble sale.

Peter, the octogenarian, wears his spectacles on the end of his nose and looks like an absent-minded professor.

Wisdom comes only with experience, after we have suffered many set-backs in life.

Three coffees, please, and two scones, and give the

bill to my friend, John, the one over there with the Russian hat.

Who was taken prisoner by the Indian chief yesterday?

Certainly not; you may not borrow your father's car. Anyway, it's not his to lend.

Think carefully. A whole company of actors depends on your decision for their future.

Comment

'Choose'	– imperative
'jumble sale'	– one entity
'after'	– adv. conjunction
'please'	– in full = 'if it please you', hence: verb 'to please', active, 3rd pers. sing., impersonal, present subj.
'the one over there' –	= 'the one who is over there' hence 'over' and 'there' are adverbs
'prisoner'	– in apposition to 'who'

Exercise 64

Where God has His church, the devil will have his chapel.

After peace had been declared, the army gradually came back to Britain, the land all the soldiers longed to see.

Several students will arrive on the first bus, if it ever does arrive in this storm.

The Lancashire archers will be shooting at the butts over by the fence.

The DC10 should normally have been arriving at Gatwick about now.

The newspaper reported that the Queen Mother's favourite programme was Mrs Dale's Diary, but no one remembers that now.

It is said that she who finds herself between two stools soon falls on the ground.

Buying new clothes was Dorothy's idea of heaven.

Rule, Britannia, Britannia rules the waves; Britons never never never shall be slaves.

The silly child fell asleep clutching his box of toys.

Comment

'land'	– in apposition to 'Britain'
'to see'	– object of 'longed'
'over by'	– treat as compound preposition
'about'	– adv. of degree modifying adv. 'now'
'Mrs Dale's Diary'	– treat as one entity
'buying'	– subject of 'was' with own object, 'clothes'
'rule'	– imperative
'Britannia'	– apostrophized. Formerly known as the 'vocative' case
'slaves'	– complement to 'shall be'
'fell asleep'	– verb 'to fall asleep'

Exercise 65

A beautifully decorated antique cheese-dish sat most strikingly on Cousin Ethel's sideboard.

'Is this yours?' the customs officer asked me.

By hitting two sixes in the final over, John managed to save his side from defeat.

Betty, my little sister, was lost in the ruins of Bolton Abbey and we could not find her for hours.

The artist painted a better likeness of my mother than if it had been a photograph of her.

If I were you, I would not think of going into that place at this time of night.

Speed delights Pat, and if he's not very careful it

may kill him one of these days.

I don't for the life of me know why they call them 'soft drinks', unless the people who drink them are soft in the head!

I shall ask Tom home for tea, but I wager you he won't accept.

We were told not to count our chickens before they are hatched.

Comment

'hitting'	– gerund, acc., gov. by 'by' with own object 'sixes' (noun)
'than if'	– 'than' = conjunction 'if' = adverbial conjunction
'(If I) were (you)'	– subjunctive. Verb is 'to think of'
'one'	– a kind of numeral pronoun, one of these days

Exercise 66

Watching the blacksmith, old Johnny Irons, shoeing the horse, Farmer Meredith suddenly remembered the days of his youth.

'Will you give me a good reference before I leave the company?' the secretary asked her boss.

Hit by a stray bullet, the lame donkey brayed out his last sad cry.

Teaching maths to pupils is quite easy if you have a class of geniuses.

In my experience radiators always leak; either you turn them off and freeze or leave them alone and mop up the gathering lake.

Matilda wore a pure cashmere cardigan, much more gorgeous than the one Pauline was wearing.

The poor Spanish lad will probably have been collected from Reading station by now; make sure his supper is ready.

Walking the dog every night was Graham's punishment for buying the wretched animal in the first
place.

Comment
'Johnny Irons' and 'shoeing' both refer to 'blacksmith'
'hit'   – past participle, qual. 'donkey'
'brayed out' –   verb = 'to bray out'
'teaching'   – gerund, subject of 'is', with own obj.,
                 'maths'
Notice the verbs:
'you turn off' 'you freeze' 'you leave alone' and 'you
mop'
'much'   – adv. of degree
Verb = 'will have been collected'
'by now'   – a tempting solution here is to regard
                 these two words as a 'compound
                 adverb'. Alternatively, 'now' is adver-
                 bial and 'by' modifies it. A third choice
                 will consider 'by' to be a preposition.

Exercise 67
(In these sentences, some 'understood' words have to
be supplied.)

Saying is one thing and doing another.
Ready money will away.
Rain before seven, fine before eleven.
In trust is treason.
Grasp all, lose all.
Least talk, most work.
Long absent, soon forgotten.
New lord, new laws.
Past cure, past care.
Soon learnt, soon forgotten.

Comment
The important thing in Exercise 67 is not to explain the meaning of the sayings, but to flesh out the grammatical skeletons.

Saying is one thing and doing 'is' another.

Ready money will 'vanish' away.

'If we have' rain before seven, 'it will be' fine before eleven.

In 'the' trust 'we place in people, there' is 'the possibility of' treason.

'If you try to' grasp all, 'you may' lose all.

'The' least talk 'you indulge in, the most work 'you will do'.

'If people are' long absent, 'they are' soon forgotten.

'When you have a' new lord, 'you will have' new laws.

'What is thought to be' past cure will be 'past care'.

'Things that are' soon learnt 'are' soon forgotten.

When you have completed these phrases, you can more easily parse the words that are left.

PART III:
ANALYSIS OF SENTENCES

In this part, we consider in detail the analysis of sentences, analyse the interweaving of clauses to form complex sentences and give examples to increase your understanding of this fascinating study of the application of elementary logic to grammar.

It can be omitted without detriment to the general study of parsing, but it is designed to give you the confidence that comes from mastery of this fundamental study of language.

Analysis

In **analysis**, we are dealing with the form of the whole sentence, in the way its separate parts fit together. Single words no longer engage our attention, although some of them act as markers.

Let us take a sentence as an example:

As they watched the plane take off, Adam and Mary felt sad to see their daughter, Sarah, who had never before been away from home for more than a couple of nights, fly off to her new life in Australia.

Here, we can separate the 'parts' of this sentence without much difficulty.

1. As they watched the plane take off
2. Adam and Mary felt sad to see their daughter Sarah . . . fly off to her new life in Australia
3. who had never before been away from home for more than a couple of nights.

The business of analysis is to relate these parts to each other, to identify their dependence. It is not difficult to see that

1. tells us **when** Adam and Mary felt sad
2. Adam . . . Australia is the **main** statement, and
3. tells us something about Sarah; it **describes** her.

Groups of words which tell us **when** are **adverbial**, and, in this sentence, 'As they watched the plane take off' tells us **when** the parents felt sad. It is therefore an **adverbial clause**, modifying the verb 'felt'.

Describing words are **adjectival**, and the clause, 'who had never been away from home for more than a couple of nights', telling us something about Sarah, is an **adjectival** clause, qualifying 'Sarah'.

The remaining clause, 'Adam . . . Australia', is the **main clause**, **main** because it is not dependent on the others.

The clues, (or markers), to watch for in an analysis are the **finite verbs**. Whenever one of these occurs, there will be a **clause**, but the verb must be **finite**.

<u>Remember</u>

Types of **sentences**
  Simple, with one main clause
  Compound, with two or more main clauses
  Complex, with a main clause and subordinate clauses

Types of **clauses**
  Main
  Subordinate – Noun, adjectival, adverbial

Clauses are identified by **finite** verbs.

Exercise 68
Identify the **finite** verbs in these sentences.

The man brought me a book to read.
Come into the warm kitchen to keep out of the cold.
You need to rest your feet after walking so far.
Singing like a bird, the little girl was happy to be left alone.

I'm not the caretaker. I'm the Headmaster.

The driver would have been killed skidding on that greasy road.

Is Jessie at home later tonight washing her hair?

To go fishing or cycling were John's favourite hobbies.

Paris and London are two wonderful places to visit.

Stacked behind that curtain are all the shopkeeper's favourite items.

Comment (F = finite, NF = non-finite)
  brought (F), to read (NF)
  come (F), to keep (NF)
  need (F), to rest (NF), walking (NF)
  singing (NF), was (F), to be left (NF)
  I'm = I am (F) x 2
  would have been killed (F), skidding (NF)
  is (F), washing (NF)
  to go fishing (NF), cycling (= to go cycling) (NF), were (F)
  are (F), to visit (NF)
  stacked (NF), are (F)

In the next exercises, the finite verbs are in italics. Write out the **clauses** to which these verbs belong; e.g.

  John *came* home to see if his sister *was* in.
'came' – John came home to see
'was'   – if his sister was in

  The man that I *saw smiled* mysteriously.
'saw'   – that I saw
'smiled' – The man . . . smiled mysteriously

Exercise 69
  The woman *told* her daughter she *should not cry* over her loss.

When the ship *docked*, the Captain *warned* the crew
    not to go ashore.

If I *come* home late, I *expect* you to be in bed.

The old tramp *stole* a loaf of bread after the woman
    had given him a cup of tea.

Don't bang the door each time you *come* in.

While the police *were searching* the house, the thief
    was climbing out of the window.

Several times I *tried*, but I *couldn't open* the umbrella.

As the plane *landed*, the fire-engines *rushed* to its
    side.

Sit down, keep quiet, *don't move* and *I'll get* your
    supper before your father *comes* in. (**Who** is to sit
    down, etc?)

He *is* a clown, and when he *is* on stage he *is* very
    funny.

Comment

'The woman told her daughter' 'that she should not
    cry . . .'

'When the ship docked' 'the Captain . . . ashore'

'If I come home late' 'I expect . . . bed'

'The old tramp . . . bread' 'after the woman . . .
    tea'

'Don't bang the door each time' 'you come in'

'While the police . . . house' 'the thief . . . window'

'Several times I tried' 'but I couldn't . . . umbrella'

'As the plane landed' 'the fire-engines . . . side'

'Sit down' 'keep quiet' 'don't move' 'and I'll . . .
    supper' 'before your father comes in'

'He is a clown' 'and when . . . stage' 'he is . . .
    funny'.

Exercise 70

The Japanese *sold* more cars in England last year
    than they *did* in France.

The farmer *said* the harvest *was* good this year.

If I *am* late, and I *might be*, especially if there *is* a strike, *see* that you *take* the dog for a walk.

Yesterday Harry *tidied* the garden, *mowed* the lawn, *cut* the hedge and *watered* the vegetables.

You *told* me you *were going* to see if there *was* any room on the beach.

That*'s* a lovely boat, and I *shall buy* it if ever I *am* rich.

You *can't run* up that hill, *it's* much too steep.

Your uncle *won't disturb* the baby or *make* a noise, *will* he?

Either the doorbell *rang* or my ears *are playing* tricks on me.

The miners *went* on strike because they *said* their wages *were* too low.

Comment

'The Japanese . . . year' 'than . . . France'

'The farmer said' 'the harvest . . . year'

'If I am late' 'and I might be' 'especially . . . strike' 'see' 'that . . . walk'

'Yesterday . . . garden' 'mowed the lawn' 'cut the hedge' 'and watered . . . vegetables'

'You told me' 'you were going to see' 'if . . . beach'

'That's . . . boat' 'and I shall buy it' 'if . . . rich'

'You . . . hill' 'it's . . . steep'

'Your uncle . . . baby' 'or . . . noise' 'will he?'

'Either . . . rang' 'or . . . me'

'The miners' 'went on strike' 'because their wages were too low' 'they said'.

Exercise 71

The yellow car that *was parked* outside all day yesterday *was towed away* this afternoon.

Babies *die* in Africa, where they *are* short of rain,

because there *are* no doctors to help them.

Although the clouds *were* black, it *did not rain* until evening, and then it *poured* down.

Did you know that the bridge we *crossed* this morning *collapsed* one hour after we *had been* there?

The soldiers *captured* several of the enemy, who *had been hiding* in the jungle, before they *returned* to camp.

Tell him that if he *doesn't turn* the volume down on his stereo, *I'll alter* the shape of his handsome face.

The Council *decided* that as the road *was* so busy they *would erect* a barrier that *would prevent* any accidents.

Last week, when the comet *passed* near the earth, some people *thought* it *would crash* into us.

The prize rose, which Mr Jones *called* 'Fair Amelia', *was chosen* because it *had* such a beautiful colour.

I'm John, *she's* Julia, and that thing over there, *who's* busy scratching his head, *is* our baby brother, Marmaduke.

Comment

'That yellow . . . yesterday' 'was . . . afternoon'

'Babies . . . Africa' 'where . . . rain' 'because . . . them'

'Although . . . black' 'it . . . evening' 'and . . . down'

'Did you know' 'that the bridge collapsed one hour' 'we crossed this morning' 'after we had been there'

'The soldiers . . . enemy' 'who . . . jungle' 'before . . . camp'

'Tell him' 'that I'll alter the shape of his handsome face' 'if he doesn't turn the volume down on his stereo'

'The Council decided' 'that they would erect a

barrier' 'as the road was so busy' 'that . . . accidents'

'Last week, some people thought' 'when . . . earth' 'it . . . us'

'The prize rose was chosen' 'which . . . Amelia' 'because . . . colour'

'I'm John' 'she's Julia' 'and that thing over there is Marmaduke' 'who's . . . head'

Adjectival Clauses

A clause which describes or qualifies a noun or pronoun is called an **adjectival clause**. Here are some examples:

> They gave him a book which had a red cover.
>> (What kind of book?)
>
> The man who was knocked down by a car was a famous singer.
>> (Which particular man?)
>
> He who crosses the tape first will receive £100.
>> (Which 'he'?)

Note: An adjectival clause always describes a word in another clause.

Exercise 72
Identify the **adjectival clauses** in these sentences and say which word or words (nouns or pronouns) they qualify.

The lightning struck the old oak which had stood there for a hundred years.

I gave my ice-cream to the little girl who was wearing the yellow dress.

Can I have my pencil back that you borrowed last week?

The Peters family went up the Eiffel Tower, which I could see from my bedroom.

They've sold the car that's been standing in the yard for weeks.

He was tried before a jury that had no knowledge of his past crimes.

The library advertised a sale of books that they no
longer wanted.

The music they played was my favourite symphony.

She was terrified of things that went bump in the
night.

Comment

'struck'	'which *had stood* there for a hundred years' qualifying 'oak'
'gave'	'who *was wearing* the yellow dress' qualifying 'girl'
'can have'	'that you *borrowed* last week' qualifying 'pencil'
'went'	'which I *could see* . . . bedroom' qualifying 'Eiffel Tower'
'sold'	'that*'s been standing* . . . yard for weeks' qualifying 'car'
'tried'	'that *had* no knowledge . . . crimes' qualifying 'jury'
'advertised'	'that they no longer *wanted*' qualifying 'books'
'was'	'they *played*' qualifying 'music'
'was terrified'	'that *went bump* in the night' qualifying 'things'

Exercise 73

Alexander Fleming helped to discover penicillin,
which cured many people's infections.

The supper they ate in that restaurant made them
ill.

People who live in the country are supposed to enjoy
peace and quiet.

Nations that have long coastlines need a strong
navy.

Sam bought a torch that had a special long-distance
beam.

Have you seen the Houses of Parliament, where all the debates take place?

Is the doctor you told me about really so very good?

There's that odd man who talks to himself all the time.

He who laughs last laughs loudest.

The explanation they gave to the teacher did not convince him.

Comment

'helped to discover'	'which *cured* . . . infections' qualifying 'penicillin'
'made'	'they *ate*' qualifying 'supper'
'are supposed'	'who *live* in the country' qualifying 'people'
'need'	'that *have* long coastlines' qualifying 'nations'
'bought'	'that *had* . . . beam' qualifying 'torch'
'have seen'	'where . . . *take place*' qualifying 'Houses of Parliament'
'Is'	'you *told* me about' qualifying 'doctor'
'There's'	'who *talks* . . . time' qualifying 'man'
'laughs'	'who *laughs* last' qualifying 'he'
'convince'	'they *gave* to the teacher' qualifying 'explanation.'

EXPANSION OF SENTENCES

Sentences can be expanded by describing one of the nouns or pronouns they contain. E.g.

The soldier put on his boots.

The soldier put on the boots he had just cleaned.

My aunt came to visit us.
My aunt, who lives in Birmingham, came to visit us.

Expand these sentences in this way. Make sure your **adjectival clause** contains a **finite verb**.

Exercise 74
The boy gave his friend one of the sweets.
Jean came home with me for tea.
London is a very noisy city.
The postman handed us the letter.
Tell me about the book.
Everyone has a secret.
The jeweller was taken to hospital.
The man's appeal for mercy was refused.
Napoleon was exiled to St Helena.
I told Peter to meet me at the station.

Comment
(These answers are, of course, only suggestions.)

'sweets'	– that he had just bought.
'Jean'	– who is my favourite cousin . . .
'London'	– which is the capital of England . . .
'letter'	– we had been expecting.
'book'	– you have been reading.
'secret'	– that they won't tell anyone else.
'jeweller'	– who was attacked in his shop . . .
'mercy'	– which was recommended by the jury . . .
'Napoleon'	– who had conquered nearly the whole of Europe . . .
'station'	– which was only a mile from our house.

Adverbial Clauses

A clause which functions like an adverb and modifies a word in another clause is called an **adverbial clause**. These clauses operate like single adverbs and modify words, usually verbs, in respect of time, place, manner, reason, condition, etc.

Here are some examples:

They went to work *after the bus dropped them at the gate*.
(Answers the question 'When did they go to work?' Adverbial clause of **time**)

He will be remembered *as he deserves to be*.
(Answers the question 'How will he be remembered?' Adverbial clause of **manner**)

The garden will be drenched *because it has been raining all night*.
(Answers the question 'Why will the garden be drenched?' Adverbial clause of **reason**)

If the train arrives on time, Mr Brown will make his connection.
(Expresses the condition 'The train will arrive if . . .' Adverbial clause of **condition**)

Exercise 75
Identify the **adverbial clauses**, say what **kind** they are and state which **verbs** they modify.

I shall come and say goodnight after you've got into bed.

When the decorator finishes, Father will lay a new carpet.

The car reached the airport on time, even though the traffic was slow.

The whole school was punished because the culprit would not own up.

Grandpa likes Susie more than he likes Tom.

If we don't have more sunshine, the harvest will be poor this year.

The miser locked up his safe whenever he left the house.

Because the sea looked calm, John ventured much too far out for safety.

Even though Mrs Watts was in such poor health, the doctor allowed her to go on holiday.

The builder will repair the roof as well as he can in the circumstances.

Comment

'after you've got into bed'	– modifies 'say' (**time**)
'when the decorator finishes'	– 'will lay' (**time**)
'even though the traffic was slow'	– 'reached' (**concession**)
'because the culprit . . . own up'	– 'punished' (**reason**)
'than he likes Tom'	– 'more' (**comparison**)
'If we don't . . . sunshine'	– 'don't have' (**condition**)
'whenever he left the house'	– 'locked up' (**time**)
'because the sea looked calm'	– 'ventured' (**reason**)
'even though . . . poor health'	– 'allowed' (**concession**)
'as well as he can . . . circumstances'	– 'will repair' (**manner**).

Exercise 76

Your little sister can run as fast as you can.

As soon as he went into the dentist's surgery, Bill's pain disappeared.

The ship had to leave harbour immediately, as the tide was running out.

If the aircraft climbs any higher, its wings will ice over.

The sunflowers next door are much taller than ours are.

I shall send you a postcard when I reach Washington.

Because the milkman was late, we had to have our tea black!

The government will send in the troops if the strike lasts any longer.

The child's handwriting was as hopeless as any the mistress had seen.

The man died before the ambulance arrived.

Comment

'as you can'	– 'as fast' (**manner/ comparison**)
'as soon . . . surgery'	– 'disappeared' (**time**)
'as the tide . . . running out'	– 'Immediately' (**reason**)
'if the aircraft . . . higher'	– 'will ice' (**condition**)
'than ours are'	– 'taller' (**comparison**)
'when I reach Washington'	– 'send' (**time**)
'Because the milkman . . . late'	– 'had' (**reason**)
'if the strike . . . longer'	– 'will send' (**condition**)
'as any . . . seen'	– 'as hopeless' (**comparison**)
'before the ambulance arrived'	– 'died' (**time**)

Exercise 77

Add an **adverbial clause** to these sentences in the
mode indicated:

Parliament met today. (**time**)
I shall join the army. (**condition**)
The Dutchman will have to return home. (**reason**)
The boy rushed into the house. (**manner**)
We shall take our holidays this year. (**place**)
Tell John I waited for him last night. (**time**)
Henry bought the book. (**reason**)
You had better buy something else. (**condition**)
Jo Punchem still decided he would fight the cham-
pion. (**concession**)
She bought a new dress. (**time**)

Noun Clauses

As a part of speech, a **noun** can be

a subject
the object of a verb
governed by a preposition
in apposition to another noun or pronoun
a complement to a verb.

Noun clauses can assume all of these roles. E.g.

As a **subject:**
That the prisoner was guilty was obvious to everyone.
(What was obvious? = subject of verb 'was obvious')
How he ever reached here will always be a mystery.
(What will be a mystery? = subject of verb 'will always be')

As an **object** of a verb:
The Captain decided *it was time to launch the torpedo.*
(What did the Captain decide?)
That white line shows *how far you can go.*
(What does the line show?)

Governed by a **preposition:**
By '*this must be done today*', he really means any time tomorrow!
(By what . . . ?)
Parliament's decision depends on *when the next election takes place.*
(On what . . . ?)

As a clause in **apposition**:

The statement *that the ship had sunk* proved to be false.

(The statement = 'that . . . sunk')

The report *that she died last night* was true.

(The report = 'that she died last night')

As a **complement**:

This is unquestionably *what the doctor ordered*.

(This = 'what the doctor ordered')

It will always be *what Tom wanted it to be*.

(It = 'what Tom wanted it to be')

Exercise 78

Identify the **noun clauses** and say what type they are:

Whether he ever returns home is the thing that worries me.

My friend agreed it was unnecessary to drive so fast.

Between 'I don't know' and 'I'm not sure' there isn't much difference in a court of law.

The announcement that Rita had had a baby girl was received with joy.

This is obviously the best he could do.

By 'be here at nine o'clock sharp' he means business.

The statement that the bank rate would not change reassured the money market.

What is important to John is not necessarily important to me.

The girl's success showed that she had courage.

It is fair to assume that he will gain university entrance without much difficulty.

Comment

'Whether . . . home'   – subject of 'is'
'it was . . . fast'   – complement to 'agreed'

'"I don't know" and "I'm not sure"' – preposition 'between'

'that Rita . . . girl' – apposition to 'announcement'

'the best . . . do' – complement to 'this'

'"be here . . . sharp"' – preposition 'by'

'that the bank . . . change' – apposition to 'statement'

'what is . . . John' – subject of 'is'

'that she had courage' – object of 'showed'

'To assume . . . difficulty' – apposition to 'it'

Exercise 79

That rich nations are reluctant to share their wealth is a well-known fact.

With 'I don't care about you', the angry woman left the house.

That is what the policeman told me.

The boy's remark that he was finished with them all left his friends very miserable.

Which play we go to see will depend on the availability of tickets.

The signpost indicated which was the road for Canterbury.

It is nonsense what he says about the fire.

From 'The Mayor desires your company at the Annual Ball', I take it that we shall have to go.

Which coat you wear is a matter for you to choose.

The waiter showed him which were the correct knife and fork to use.

Comment

'That rich . . . wealth'   – subject of 'is'

'"I don't care about you"'   – preposition 'with'
'what the policeman told me' – complement to 'that'
'that he had . . . all'   – apposition to 'remark'
'which play . . . see'   – subject of 'depend'
'which was . . . Canterbury' – object of 'indicated'
'what he says . . . fire'   – apposition to 'nonsense'
'"The Mayor . . . Ball"'   – preposition 'from'
'which coat you wear'   – subject of 'is'
'which were . . . to use'   – object of 'showed'

Exercise 80
Change the phrases in italics into **noun clauses**.

The teacher was sorry to learn *of his failure to pass the exam*.

One man's meat is another man's poison.

The swimmer shouted to the onlookers *to come to his help*.

Ask me *for my address*.

The soldier's burial place was never revealed to his family.

London wanted to know *Moscow's answer*.

This is *his destination*.

Not allowing anyone to pass is the regiment's motto.

The milkman said *something about leaving two extra pints*.

Mission Control's message was *about the Challenger's being launched the next day*.

Comment
'that he had failed to pass the exam'
'The meat that one man eats'
'that they should come to his help'
'where I live' or 'what my address is'
'Where the soldier was buried'
'what Moscow's answer was'

'where he was going'
'They shall not pass'
'that he would leave two extra pints'
'that the Challenger would be launched the next day'

Note: These are, of course, only suggested answers.
The important point is that the clause must contain a
finite verb.

Main Clauses

These can be deceptive. Sometimes short and apparently conveying little information, main clauses are identified by the fact that they are not dependent on, or subordinate to, any other clause-unit in the same sentence. Generally, there are three steps:

1. identify the finite verbs
2. group the words that form the clauses
3. sift the subordinate ones from the main clause.

   E.g.

As the inspector left the station he said he was happy that he had solved the case.

'left'   – As the Inspector left the station . . .
'said'   – he said . . .
'was'   – (that) he was happy . . .
'had solved'– that he had solved the case.

It will be seen that of the four clauses

A. 'As the Inspector left the station . . .' tells us **when** he said something
B. (that) 'he was happy' . . . tells us **what** he said, and
C. 'that he had solved the case' . . . tells us **why** he was happy.

In other words, these three clauses relate to other clauses in the sentence. The only one which stands independent is 'he said . . .', and this is the **main clause**.

A. is an **adverbial clause of time** modifying 'said'
B. is a **noun clause**, object of 'said'
C. is an **adverbial clause of reason** modifying 'was happy'.

Here is another example.

> The concert which took place in the Royal Festival Hall, where the ambassadors had gathered, was interrupted when the bomb scare sounded.

A. 'took place'   – which took place in the R.F.H.
B. 'had gathered'   – where the ambassadors had gathered
C. 'was interrupted' – The concert . . . was interrupted
D. 'sounded'   – as the bomb scare sounded.

Here three of the clauses, A, B and D, show evidence of subordination:

A. is an **adjectival clause** qualifying 'concert',
B. is another **adjectival clause**, descriptive of the R.F.H., 'in which the ambassadors had gathered'
D. is an **adverbial clause of time** telling us **when** the concert was interrupted.

This leaves us with C, the **main clause**: 'The concert . . . was interrupted', which is not subordinate to any of the others.

Note: Link words sometimes provide clues. 'Which', 'where', 'when', 'as' and 'that' will *probably* introduce subordinate clauses.

Exercise 81
Identify all the **clauses** in these sentences and describe their functions in detail.

As the yacht which he had just bought sailed into the harbour, Captain O'Hoythere swelled with pride.

Whether or not the bank manager will give us a loan is the big question.

Before Jenkins captained the team, but after they won the Derby Cup, Range Rovers XI were a very fine side.

The money I borrowed from Bob was stolen from my bag when I was mugged last night.

Did you say Mr Robbins telephoned twice and no one was in to answer him?

Mary, if she ever gets there, promised to call at the chemist where your prescription is awaiting collection.

It is the summer that upsets me when there is no water and the crops are all dried up before we can harvest them.

Go away until Father comes home; then he will deal with you.

As the House of Lords ended their sitting, the intruder, who had hidden in the gallery, fired three shots and killed the Lord Chancellor and a clerk who had been sitting next to him.

I once read in a book that the writer had an uncle who distrusted all people from the East ever since he bought a ticket that failed to win the Calcutta Sweep.

Comment

'As the yacht . . . sailed into the harbour'	– **adv. time** mod. swelled'
'which . . . bought'	– **adj.** qual. 'yacht'
'Captain O'Hoythere . . . pride'	– **main**
'Whether . . . loan'	– **noun**, subj. of 'is'
'is . . . question'	– **main**

'Before . . . team'	– **adv.** **time** mod. 'were'
'but after . . . Cup'	– **adv.** **time** mod. 'were'
'Range Rovers . . . side'	– **main**
'The money . . . was stolen . . . bag'	– **main**
'I borrowed from Bob'	– **adj.** qual. 'money'
'when . . . mugged'	– **adv. time** mod. 'was stolen'
'Did you say'	– **main**
'Mr Robbins . . . twice'	– **noun,** obj. of 'did say'
'and no one . . . him?'	– **noun,** obj. of 'did say'
'Mary . . . promised to call . . . chemist'	– **main**
'if she . . . there'	– **adv.** **cond.** mod. 'promised'
'where . . . collection'	– **adj.** qual. 'chemist'
'It is the summer'	– **main**
'that upsets me'	– **adj.** qual. 'summer'
'when . . . water'	– **adv. time** mod. 'is'
'and (when) the crops . . . up'	– **adv. time** mod. 'is'
'before . . . them'	– **adv. time** mod. 'are dried up'
'Go away'	– **main**
'until . . . home'	– **adv. time** mod. 'Go away'
'then . . . you'	– **adv.** **time** mod. 'comes'
'As the . . . sitting'	– **adv.** **time** mod. 'fired'

'the intruder . . . fired three shots'	– **main**
'and (he) killed . . . clerk'	– **main**
'who . . . gallery'	– **adj.** qual. 'intruder'
'who had been . . . to him'	– **adj.** qual. 'clerk'

'I once . . . book'	– **main**
'That . . . uncle'	– **noun,** obj. of 'read'
'who . . . East'	– **adj.** qual. 'uncle'
'ever since . . . ticket'	– **adv. time** mod. 'distrusted'
'that failed . . . Sweep'	– **adv.** qual. 'ticket'

Exercise 82

If England bats first, they will win unless the Aussies strike a lucky patch.

This is how the seagull does it: swooping low, it snatches the fish just as it nears the surface.

If the coalman brings some coal today, that will be the answer to our problem.

Whenever I visit the zoo, especially the one at Chester, I see all my relatives jumping up and down in their cages.

I told him because first, he already knew and, second, Jane said she was going to tell him tomorrow anyway.

'Which dress do you like?' Sally asked her friend as they looked in the shop window.

One thing you can say if you are an actor, if the audience is booing you, at least you can say they're still there.

Heaven grant me that my prayer comes true and our maths master will have a stomach-ache tomorrow and won't be here to collect any homework.

Unhappy is the man who envies what other people have.

What people have never worries me because I'm not jealous of others.

Comment

'If England . . .'	adv. cond., main, adv. cond.
'This is how . . .'	main, noun comp., main, adv. time
'If the coalman . . .'	noun app., main
'Whenever I visit . . .'	adv. time, main
'I told him . . .'	main, adv. reason, adv. reason
'"Which dress . . ."'	noun obj., main, adv. time
'One thing . . .'	main, adv. cond., adv. cond., main, noun obj.
'Heaven grant me . .'	main, noun obj., noun obj., noun obj.
'Unhappy is the . . .'	main, adj., noun obj.
'What people have . . .'	noun subj., main, adv. reason

Exercise 83

Robert Benchley, who was an old-fashioned gentleman, when he first bought a car, could not help remarking that he found it difficult to knock a woman down and not feel unchivalrous about it.

When he visited Cornwall, Tim was fascinated by the ocean that seemed so vast that he was frightened by it.

Although people make a great fuss over them, dogs are neglected by those who should know better.

Elizabeth thought grown-ups looked untidy and she said they walked about as though their legs and arms weren't joined on properly.

Anything you can do, I can do better.

If I am a great man who governs the lives of thousands of people, many of my friends are frauds.

George was not always wrong, but he had the habit of always being wrong at the right time.

That my memory is going is something I have

learned to live with, but I still wish I could remember what that woman's name is.

It is reported that when General Brabazon arrived at his village station and the porter told him his train had just left, he said, 'Then bring another!'

Shakespeare, in one of his famous plays, divided men into those who are born great, those who achieve greatness and those who have greatness thrust upon them, but he never foresaw the time when men would hire press secretaries to make themselves look great.

Comment

'Robert Benchley . . . could . . . remarking'	**main**
'who was . . . gentleman'	**adj.** qual. 'R.B.'
'when he . . . car'	**adv. time** mod. 'could help'
'that he . . . woman down'	**noun,** obj. of 'remarking'
'and . . . about it'	**noun,** obj. of 'remarking'
'When he visited . . .'	– **adv. time, main, adj., adv. reason**
'Although people . . .'	– **adv. concess., main, adj.**
'Elizabeth thought . . .'	– **main, noun obj., main, noun obj., adv. manner**
'Anything you . . .'	– **noun obj., main**
'If I am a great . . .'	– **adv. cond., adj., main**
'George was not . . .'	– **main**
'That my memory . . .'	– **noun subj. main, noun app. main, noun obj., noun obj.**

'It is reported'	– **main**
'that . . . he said'	– **noun,** obj. of 'reported'
'when General . . . station'	– **adv. time** mod. 'said'
'and (when) the porter . . . left'	– **adv. time** mod. 'said'
'"Then bring another!"'	– **noun,** obj. of 'said'
'Shakespeare . . . divided men . . . those'	– **main**
'in . . . plays'	– **adv. time** mod. 'wrote'
'who are born great'	– **adj.** qual. 'those'
'(those) who . . . greatness'	– **adj.** qual. 'those'
'and . . . upon them'	– **adj.** qual. 'those'
'but he . . . time'	– **main**
'when men . . . great'	– **adj.** qual. 'time'

Final revision exercises

Parsing

Exercise 84
Parse the words in italics in these sentences.

1. '*Italian* food *doesn't suit* my *horde* of *savages*,' said the teacher *as* she *gave out medicine* to the pupils *suffering from stomach pains*.
2. '*Those* cars *must be sold* by the *end* of the month,' the manager *said, looking at all* the *unsold* vehicles *cluttering up his compound*.
3. We *had been expecting* Tommy *to arrive last* Wednesday, *but apparently* he *had not even thought of coming until* we phoned *him* on *Friday*.
4. A *group* of women *had begun* the *disturbance, complaining about their* treatment, and they *were soon joined* by the men in the *other* part of the *factory*.

5. *Roast* beef and *Yorkshire pudding are my idea* of a *Sunday* lunch, *followed* by a large *ice-cream* and a *sleep.*

6. *Descartes* said, 'I *think, therefore* I *am' only* he said *it* in Latin, and it *sounds much more impressive like that.*

7. My mother *says that when* I think I *scratch* my head, but she *doesn't mind because* she *picks up* the *splinters* and *lights* the fire *with them.*

8, I saw *this* man go up to the *lamp-posts, raise his* hat and say *good-morning to them,* and *then I* felt *my* Dad *shaking me, saying.* 'Stop *dreaming, lazybones, it's time to get up.'*

9. *As* the aircraft *swooped down out* of the clouds, the *whole* panorama of the *countryside was spread out below,* and *it* looked *so peaceful* and *fertile.*

Comment

Note: These are not complete answers. Full parsing is left to you. Here, only the part of speech is identified.

1. Italian – adj.	(doesn't suit – does not suit)
horde – noun	(= verb (does suit) + Adv (not))
savages – noun	as — adv. conj.
gave out – verb	medicine – noun
suffering – participle	from – prep.
stomach – adj.	pains – noun
2. Those – adj.	must be sold – verb
end – noun	said – verb
looking – participle	at – prep.
all – adj.	unsold – adj.
cluttering up – participle	his – adj.
compound – noun	

3. had been expecting – verb   to arrive – infinitive
   last – adj.   but – conj.
   apparently – adv.   had not even thought –
   of – prep.   (had thought – verb)
   coming – gerund   (not – adv. even – adv.)
   until – adv./conj.   him – pron.
   Friday – noun

4. group – noun   had begun – verb
   disturbance – noun   complaining – participle
   about – prep.   their – adj.
   (were soon joined –)   other – adj.
   (were joined – verb)   factory – noun
   (soon – adv.)

5. Roast – adj.   Yorkshire – adj.
   pudding – noun   are – verb
   my – adj.   idea – noun
   Sunday – adj.   followed – participle
   ice-cream – noun   sleep – noun

6. Descartes – noun   think – verb
   therefore – adv.   am – verb
   only – adv.   it – pron.
   sounds – verb   much – adv.
   more impressive – adv.   like – prep.
   that – pron.

7. says – verb   that – conj.
   doesn't mind – verb+adv.   because – adv./conj.
   picks up – verb   splinters – noun
   lights – verb   with – prep.
   them – pron.

8. this – adj.   lamp-posts – noun
   raise – infinitive   his – adj.
   good-morning – noun   them – pron.
   then – adv./conj.   I – pron.
   my – adj.   shaking – gerund

me – pron.
Stop – verb
lazybones – noun
time – noun

saying – participle
dreaming – gerund
it's – it is = pron.+verb
to get up – infinitive

9. As – adv./conj.
down – adv.
whole – adj.
was spread out – verb
it – pron.
peaceful – adj.

swooped – verb
out – adv.
countryside – noun
below – adv.
so – adv.
fertile – adj.

Exercise 85
Parse the words in italics in these sentences.

1. *Confidence comes* with experience.
2. *Several teams* entered the competition.
3. *That* flavour is *quite artificial.*
4. You can go out *to play,* but *be home by* six o'clock.
5. The boy *was being chased by the fiercest-looking* dog *you've ever seen.*
6. *Whose* book were you reading and *why haven't you returned it?*
7. *Give them* a sweet *each,* but *not* the *mint humbugs. They're mine.*
8. *Is that the only* coat you've got *to put on?*
9. *Norfolk* people have a *habit* of *speaking as though* they had a cold *in* the *nose.*
10. *Peace,* or *absence* of *fighting,* is *something that man has striven for throughout* the *ages.*

Comment
1. Confidence – noun   comes – verb
2. Several – adj.   teams – noun
3. that – adj.   quite – adv.
   artificial – adj.

4. to play – infinitive   but – conj.
   be – verb   home – adv.
   by – prep.   o'clock – noun
5. was being chased – verb   fiercest-looking – adj.
   you've ever seen – you have ever seen pron. +
   verb+adv.
6. whose – adj.   why – adv.
   haven't you returned – have you not returned =
   verb+pron.+adv.
   it – pron.
7. Give – verb   them – pron.
   each – pron.   not – adv.
   mint humbug – noun   they're – they are = pron.
                                  +verb
   mine – pron.
8. Is – verb   that – pron.
   the – def. art.   to put on – infinitive
9. Norfolk – adj.   habit – noun
   speaking – gerund   as though – adv./conj.
   in – prep.   nose – noun
10. Peace – noun   absence – noun
    fighting – gerund   something – pron.
    that – pron.   man – noun
    has striven for – verb   throughout – prep.
    ages – noun

Exercise 86

1. *Watching* the *animal suffer* made Helen a *life-long vegetarian.*
2. *Neither* the postman *nor* the milkman *had called* at *No. 56, so no one knew that* Mrs Sampson *had fallen down unconscious.*
3. He batted *very patiently* and, *as a result,* Lancashire *succeeded* in *holding* Sussex *to a draw.*
4. The *French* athlete, *Robert Levite,* told the *European* association *that his* country *could not*

send any more runners to *London*.

5. The girl *had been thrown against* a fence *during* the accident and *was being treated* by the *ambulance driver as* she *lay* on the pavement.

6. *What* did he say? *Whom* did he blame *Whose fault did he said it* was? *Which* hospital did *they* take *him to? When* can I see *him*?

7. A *dozen* pencils *were missing from* the *box*, and the shopkeeper thought *there might be five* or *six more also missing*.

8. *Most certainly* you *can have some* wine. I suggest the *1962 Macon* or the *1938 Chablis, except that that one* is *terribly expensive*.

9. *Having been brought* to his *senses by* the *good-talking-to* that Mary *had given* him, Charlie promised *to behave himself* in the *future*.

10. The *little* girl clapped her *hands happily when* she saw the *enormous* doll *her* mother *had brought home for her*.

Comment

1. Watching – participle   animal – noun
   suffer – infinitive   life-long – adj.
   vegetarian – noun
2. Neither – conj.   nor – conj.
   had called – verb   No. 56 – noun
   so – adv./conj.   no one – pron.
   knew – verb   that – conj.
   had fallen down – verb   unconscious – adj.
3. very – adv.   patiently – adv.
   as – prep.   result – noun
   succeeded – verb   holding – gerund
   to – prep.   draw – noun
4. French – adj.   Robert Levite – noun
   European – adj.   that – conj.

his – adj.

could not send – verb + adv.

any – adv.

more – adj.

London – noun

5. Had been thrown – verb   against – prep.

during – prep.   was being treated – verb

ambulance driver – noun   as – adv./conj.

lay – verb

6. What – pron.   whom – pron.

whose – adj.   fault – noun

did he say – verb+pron.   it – pron.

which – adj.   they – pron.

him – pron.   to – prep. (or part of verb 'to take to')

when – adv.   him – pron.

7. dozen – adj. or noun?   were missing – verb

from – prep.   box – noun

there – pron.   might be – verb

five, six – adjs.? prons.? or nouns?

more – adj. or pron.?   also – adv.

missing – participle

8. Most certainly – adj.   can have – verb

some – adj.   1962 Macon – noun

1938 Chablis – noun   except that – adv./conj.

that – adj.   one – pron.

terribly – adv.   expensive – adj.

9. Having been brought – participle

senses – noun   by – prep.

good – adj.   talking to – noun

had given – verb   to behave – infinitive

himself – pron.   future – noun

10. little – adj.   hands – noun

happily – adv.   when – adv./conj.

enormous – adj.   her – adj.

had brought – verb   home – adv.

for – prep.   her – pron.

Exercise 87
Parse the words in italics in this passage.

During my last term at school I *was* the *champion* gymnast in the *county*, and the PE master, *Jerry Hawkins, treated me as* a friend rather than a pupil. *On one* occasion he *stopped me* in the corridor *and* asked me *for my help*.

'*Your* uncle is a *theatrical* costumier, *isn't* he?' he said. *I* nodded. '*Ask* him *if* he'll lend me *an academic* robe of *some kind*. *We've been told that* we *all have to wear* our robes on *Speech Night, because* the Vice-Chancellor of Oxford University is *to be* the *guest* of *honour* and, as *you* know, I *don't own* a gown of *any sort*.'

I went *down* into my *uncle's Aladdin's Cave* of a warehouse and, *having his permission of course, parcelled up* the *most imposing* gown I *could find*, a magnificent *specimen with* white fur round the collar.

On the night of the *ceremony*, Jerry *was sitting there looking more splendid* than the Headmaster himself. *Needless to say*, I felt *very* pleased with *myself*. The *next* morning, *however*, he grabbed *me* as I came *into* school *like* a *bull mastiff*. He was in a *towering* rage. I *could not understand why*.

'*That gown!*' he exploded. '*When* the prize-giving *was over, all* the staff *went* into the *Common Room* for refreshments.' He was *almost* in tears with the *memory* of it. 'The Vice-Chancellor *spots* my gown, *ignores everyone else*, comes *hurtling* over to me, *shakes me* by the hand like a *long lost friend*, and starts *thundering away* in Latin and Greek, *expecting me* to answer him in the same *way*! I wanted *to drop down* into the bowels of the earth!'

Poor Jerry! I *had brought him* the gown of a Doctor of Letters, no less, in *Classics!*

Comment

During – prep.

was – verb

county – noun

treated – verb

as – prep.

one – adj.

me – pron.

for – prep.

help – noun

theatrical – adj.

I – pron.

if – adv./conj.

academic – adj.

kind – noun

that – conj.

to wear – infinitive

because – adv./conj.

guest – noun

you – pron.

any – adj.

down – adv.

Aladdin's cave – noun

his – adj.

of – prep.

parcelled up – verb

could find – verb

with – prep.

was sitting – verb

looking – participle

Needless – adj.

very – adv.

next – adj.

as – conj.

my – adj.

champion – noun

Jerry Hawkins – noun

me – pron.

On – prep.

stopped – verb

and – conj.

my – adj.

Your – adj.

isn't – is not = verb+adv.

Ask – verb

an – indef. art.

some – adj.

We've been told – we have been told = pron. + verb

all – pron.

Speech Night – noun

to be – infinitive

honour – noun

don't own – do not own = verb + adv.

sort – noun

uncle's – noun

having – participle

permission – noun

course – noun

most imposing – adj.

specimen – noun

ceremony – noun

there – adv.

more splendid – adj.

to say – infinitive

myself – pron.

however – adv.

into – prep.

like – prep.	bull mastiff – noun
towering – adj.	couldn't understand – could not
	understand = verb+adv.
why – pron.	That – adj.
gown – noun	When – adv./conj.
was over – verb	all – adj.
went – verb	Common Room – noun
almost – adv.	memory – noun
it – pron.	spots – verb
ignores – verb	everyone – pron.
else – adj.	hurtling – participle
shakes – verb	me – pron.
long – adv.	lost – adj.
friend – noun	thundering – participle
away – adv.	to drop – infinitive
down – adv.	Poor – adj.
Jerry – noun	had brought – verb
him – pron.	Classics – noun

Analysis

Exercise 88
List all the **finite verbs** in this passage. There are seventy-five.

'Stay in your room and don't come down until I tell you!'

Her mother's voice still rang in Emma's ears and only made her more cross. It was all because of silly Bottle. Bottle was Emma's puppy, which meant that she had to walk it, bath it, brush it, feed it and generally train it to behave itself. Well, she had forgotten to take Bottle for a walk and, of course, dear Bottle, who had the brain of a peanut, small peanut, that is, had messed all over the sitting-room floor.

Tommy could go out. Tommy, her brother, was

the apple of his mother's eye. In fact, he was the
whole basket of fruit. She wouldn't do anything to
stop Tommy enjoying himself. Emma could hear
him now, laughing and playing with his friends.
Then she spotted Maisie and Pam, her friends,
sitting on the bench just outside her house. She
called to them, they looked up and called back. She
could have happily wrung Bottle's neck for him!
Emma then had an idea. The window wasn't as high
as all that, perhaps she could climb down. Hadn't
Mr Ellis, her PE teacher, said she was a fine athlete?
She went back into the bedroom, opened the door to
listen for any noises downstairs, but there weren't
any. Closing the door, she changed into a pair of
jeans that were draped over a chair. Next, she went
over to the window again.

'I can jump that,' she thought and placed one leg
over the sill. It seemed no distance at all and who
would be any the wiser, she said to herself. Gingerly
she let herself down over the ledge so that she hung
as far as she could in order to reduce the height she
had to jump. Maisie and Pam had seen what was
happening and were coming to help. Taking a big
gasp of air – Emma thought that that was what
parachutists would do – she jumped.

Poor Emma! The pain in her ankle was terrible,
and who do you think was the first to come up to her
– Bottle! Licking her face and wagging his tail, he
jumped up and down, barking like a motor-bike that
was back-firing. None of the girls could keep him
quiet; he thought it was a great game. Of course,
Emma's mother was soon at the scene, the car was
brought round, and Emma, the champion athlete,
found herself in the casualty department of the
Hillcrest Hospital where the doctor and nurse soon
had her ankle in plaster.

Years later, Emma told the story to her friends at college, with much laughter, except that she missed Bottle. He had wanted to come to college with her, but never passed his exams. You must have guessed by now what a stupid dog he was!

Comment
Note: Elliptical phrases have not been separated out. Hence 'don't come', 'hadn't', etc. are given as **verbs**, without detaching the adverbs.

Stay   don't come down   tell   rang   made   was   was   meant   had (aux. used with infinitives 'to walk', 'bath' 'brush' 'feed' 'train' 'behave'; treat as separate verbs, conjugated with 'had' each time) had forgotten   had   is   had messed   could go out   was   was   wouldn't do   could hear   spotted called   looked   called back   could have wrung   had wasn't   could climb   hadn't said   was   went opened   weren't   changed   were draped   went   can jump   thought   placed   seemed   would be   said let down   hung   could   had   had seen   was happening   were coming   thought   was   would do jumped   was   do think   was   jumped   was backfiring   could keep   thought   was   was   was brought found   had   told   missed   had wanted   passed must have guessed   was.

Exercise 89
Write out all the **adjectival clauses** in it, saying what word(s) they describe.

Comment
'who had the brain of a peanut'   – qualifies 'Bottle'
'that were draped over a chair'   – 'jeans'
'which she had to jump'   – 'height'
'that was back-firing'   – 'motor-bike'

Exercise 90
Write out all the **adverbial clauses**, saying what word(s) they modify.

Comment

'until I tell you'	– modifies 'come down' (**time**)
'perhaps she could climb down'	– modifies previous clause (**probability**)
'so that she hung down'	– modifies 'let down' (**reason**)
'as far as she could'	– modifies 'hung' (**manner**)
'where the doctor . . . plaster'	– modifies 'found herself' (**place**)
'except that she missed Bottle'	– modifies previous clause (**concession**)

Exercise 91
Write out all the **noun clauses**, explaining their function: subject, object, complement or in apposition.

Comment

'which meant'	– in apposition to main clause ('and this meant')
'she had to walk it' (also 'had to bath' 'had to brush' 'had to feed' 'had to train')	– complement of 'which meant'
'that is'	– complement to the first 'peanut'
'she was a fine athlete'	– object of 'had said'
'I can jump that'	– object of 'thought'
'who would be any the wiser'	– object of 'said'
'what was happening'	– object of 'had seen'
'that was'	– object of 'thought'

'What parachutists would do' — complement of 'that was'

'who was the first one . . . to her' — object of 'do think'

'it was a great game' — object of 'thought'

'what a stupid dog he was' — object of 'must have guessed'

Exercise 92
In these sentences, which are the **main clauses**?

1. I said he should not attempt to drive all that way without resting.
2. Give Peter, the boy who is on his own by the deck-chair, one of the beach balls to play with.
3. Never lend any money and never borrow any, that was the advice he gave me.
4. I know you are leaving school tomorrow so we shall probably not see you again, unless you come back to see us.
5. Whatever time she decides to come, tell her I want to see her.
6. 'Come here to me, look me straight in the eye and tell me the truth,' Father said to Peter.
7. Do you think Liverpool will win the Cup again this year?
8. There are ten children in the 1st class and twelve in the 2nd who are going to France.
9. 'Who did you say was coming to the party?' I asked Bill, as he was going through his list.
10. Stop and think before you move and see if the coast is clear.

Comment
1. I said
2. Give Peter . . . one of the beach balls to play with.

3. . . . that was the advice . . .
4. I know . . .
5. . . . tell her . . .
6. . . . Father said to Peter.
7. Do you think . . .
8. There are ten children in the 1st class and twelve in the 2nd . . .
9. . . . I asked Bill . . .
10. (i) Stop (ii) think (iii) see . . .

Exercise 93

What functions (**adjectival**, **adverbial** or **noun**) do the phrases in italics serve in these sentences?

1. *Coming home late at night*, John did not expect *to find any supper*.
2. I think the actor is funny *only at the beginning of the play*.
3. The teacher gave the pupil *something to remember*.
4. *Enjoying the sun in Spain* was Susie's idea of a great holiday.
5. The book, *'As Old As The Hills'*, kept Peter amused *for the whole night*.
6. *Thinking about his new job*, Charles rushed home very excited.
7. *Thinking about his new job* nearly caused Charles an accident on the way home.
8. He'll get no work done today *thinking about his new job*.

Comment

1. Coming home late at night — adverbial, time
   to find any supper — noun, object
2. only at the beginning of the play — adverbial, time
3. something to remember — noun, object
4. Enjoying the sun in Spain — noun, subject

5. *'Old As The Hills'*   – noun, apposition
   for the whole night   – adverbial, time
6. Thinking about his new job   – adjectival
7. Thinking about his new job   – noun, subject
8. thinking about his new job   – adverbial, reason

PART IV:
ADVANCED EXERCISES IN
WORD USAGE

A number of words have been selected for this section because they are frequently used incorrectly. Examples of bad practice are given and rules are suggested to help you avoid such practices. The aim is to liberate you from the inaccuracies, the looseness of thought and the ignorance that have grown up around the everyday employment of certain words and phrases in the English language.

Ideally, you should be sure that what you are saying is correct; you should adhere to the framework of grammatical rules that has been neglected for some time; you should enjoy the confidence that mastery of parsing and syntax will give you. Nothing else can provide that.

'As'

This word can give offence in a number of ways:

'As' in place of 'because'.
The use of 'as to'.
The omission of 'as' with certain verbs.
The use of 'such as'.
'As' used as a relative pronoun or relative adverb.
The correct case after 'as'.

'AS' IN PLACE OF 'BECAUSE'

Exercise 94
Comment on the use of 'as' in these sentences.

1. As the wind was so strong she stayed at home.
2. He did not show her the way, as she was familiar with the neighbourhood.
3. Johnny Clobham still holds the title as he beat Ben Bold in the championship fight.
4. The farmers wanted an increase in milk prices as it had been a very severe winter.
5. As hunger gripped the nation, revolution followed soon after.
6. I shall not keep Harris in employment in this company as he shows no interest in the job.
7. I shall not tell you any more as you know the rest of the story.
8. Bob will have to go to Scotland as he must attend his uncle's funeral.
9. As she always came first in the class, Jenny was

presented with a special prize.
10. I don't understand what you are saying as you
    have your mouth full of chocolate.

Comment
It is good practice to use 'as', in the sense of 'because',
in two instances only:

1. When the 'as' clause comes before the main
   sentence, e.g. nos 1, 5 and 9.
2. When it follows the main sentence, 'as' can be
   used to mean 'because' if the information contained within is already known to the reader,
   e.g. nos 2 and 7.

In the remaining sentences, the use of 'as' for 'because'
is to be avoided.

THE USE OF 'AS TO'

Exercise 95
Consider these sentences.

1. As to the question of expenses, the Board will
   give you a ruling.
2. I have no idea as to his whereabouts.
3. My friend had no knowledge as to the extent of
   his responsibility for the damage.
4. The customer was very abusive as to the
   treatment she had received.
5. The Opposition would not be so foolish as to ask
   for a debate on the economic situation.
6. There is some doubt as to whether the bank will
   lend you the money.
7. The boy could not explain as to how he came to
   be so late.

8. The Met Office had no explanation as to how it came to rain so heavily at the weekend.
9. As to his request to leave early, I am afraid the Director will not hear of it.
10. She wanted to ask as to how far the relationship had already gone.

Comment
The words 'as to' are legitimately used only in nos 1, 5 and 9.

Frequently, however, they are
1. A lazy substitute for a preposition, *or*
2. A superfluous (Fowler says 'repulsive') embellishment.

Correct as follows:

2. . . . no idea **of** his whereabouts . . .
3. . . . knowledge **of** the extent . . .
4. . . . abusive **about** the treatment . . .
6. . . . some doubt whether . . . (i.e. omit)
7. . . . could not explain how . . . (omit)
8. . . . no explanation how . . . (omit)
10. . . . to ask how far . . . (omit)

THE OMISSION OF 'AS' WITH CERTAIN VERBS

Exercise 96
Consider these sentences.
1. I regarded his absence a most inconvenient as well as a most improper way to behave.
2. He observed that the main purpose of the fence was no longer a means of keeping out strangers

but a decoration around the house.

3. The lady collected old teapots – specimens that were regarded among the finest in the world.

4. The professor believed that the principal reason for the retention of corporal punishment was not just a method of retribution but an aid to better understanding of right and wrong.

5. My sister regarded Trudy, her dog, not just her own personal property but also as a status symbol among her friends.

Comment

'As' is sometimes wrongly omitted after verbs of 'regarding', 'observing' and others like them. This occurs especially when another 'as' is found in the sentence and the spectre of repetition rears its head.

1. 'I regarded his absence **as** a most inconvenient . . .

2. . . . was no longer **as** a means of . . . but **as** a decoration . . .

3. . . . that were regarded **as** among the . .

4. . . . was not just **as** a method of retribution . . . but **as** an aid . . .

5. . . . not just **as** her own . . .

THE USE OF 'SUCH AS'

Exercise 97
Consider these sentences.

1. The machine could be driven by different fuels such as petrol, gas or even electricity.

2. Some people can contribute in one way, such as, for example, by raising funds and some in

another way, such as running jumble sales.

3. My daughter was always interested in strange hobbies, such as collecting salt-pots and pill-boxes.

4. John was vitally concerned with the waifs and strays of this world, such as, for instance, the old men and women who sleep rough in big cities.

5. It was her ambition to play great Shakespearean roles such as Desdemona, Cleopatra and Juliet.

Comment

'Such as' must be followed by a noun, not a preposition, therefore:

1. The sentence is correct. By the same reasoning, so are nos 3, 4 and 5.

2. 'Such as' is followed by 'by', which is inadmissible. Omit 'such as' in both cases and substitute 'by running' for the second.

'AS' USED AS A RELATIVE PRONOUN OR RELATIVE ADVERB

Exercise 98

1. The headmaster decided to hold a sports day, as is often done during the last week of the summer term.

2. With a dash of garlic, as has been found advisable in other dishes, the pasta will be greatly improved.

3. The social worker has no power to search the flat, as is granted to the police in such circumstances.

4. Some clever clothes have come from the Savoy Fashion House, as have also come from many of the other English houses.

5. The box of chocolates he brought for his hostess was merely a courtesy, as it often is on such occasions.
6. England ought to use one of the Lancashire spinners on these occasions, as has always been effective in the past.
7. With the loss of half a stone in weight, as has always been found helpful, the boxer ought to win the fight.
8. Greece, as it is well known, was the land where democracy began.
9. The under-21s have no vote in this matter, as is possessed by the older members of the club.
10. In international finance, dealing in millions of pounds or dollars, as it is customarily done, never worries the bankers.

Comment

One of the purposes 'as' can serve is as a **relative pronoun** and another is as a **relative adverb**. Confusion between these two roles can result in mistakes.

The *relative* element of these functions links two clauses, relating the second to the first by reference to some antecedent. When 'as' is used as a relative pronoun, its antecedent is a *verb*, or *verbal idea*, or *a noun which has not been expressed but has been understood* in the main clause. If we take sentence no 1, to what does 'as' refer? Not to 'sports day', but to the idea of a 'holding', not explicitly mentioned in the main clause. The antecedent relationship is, therefore, flawed. Reword.

1. . . . to hold a sports day, as headteachers often do . . .
2. . . . of garlic, which has been found . . .
3. . . . to search the flat, as the police do . . . or

... to search the flat, a power granted to ...

4. ... Savoy Fashion House, and some also from ...

5. ... a courtesy, which it often is ...

6. ... on these occasions, as they have always been ...

7. ... in weight, which has always been found ...

8. Either ... Greece, as is well known ... or ... Greece, it is well known ...
Note: Here 'as' = 'which fact', and the construction in the original sentence is impossible.

9. A suggested reconstruction of this sentence would be: In this matter, the under-21s have no vote, as the older members alone possess it.

10. ... pounds or dollars, as is customarily done ...
Note: 'as' here is a relative adverb which introduces an adjectival clause qualifying the gerund 'dealing'.

CORRECT CASE AFTER 'AS'

What is the difference between these two sentences?
A. You like him as much as me.
B. You like him as much as I.

Exercise 99

1. John eats as much as her.
2. He works as hard as me.
3. They can't sing as well as we.
4. I ought to go to the concert as well as them.
5. He deserves the medal as much as me.
6. When such as him are rewarded, I think we should protest.
7. If criminals such as them are treated so

leniently, people will object.

8. If such as I can run three miles for charity, then surely Elizabeth and Ann can.

9. I remembered the woman as being her I had seen on a previous occasion.

10. You spoke to the soldier as him who was on duty for the Royal Birthday celebration.

Comment

A. You like him as much as me = You like me . . .
B. You like him as much as I = I like him.

In sentences where a verb can be supplied after 'as', the case should correspond accordingly:

When such as **she** die . . .
He is not as clever as **I** (am).

Hence

1. . . . as much as **she** eats.
2. . . . as hard as **I** work.
3. Correct.
4. . . . as well as **they** ought to go.
5. . . . as much as **I** deserve it.

When the provision of a verb is not possible, the case after 'as' follows the corresponding noun before 'as'. Hence:

6. When such as **he** are rewarded . . .
7. . . . criminals such as **they** . . .
8. Correct
9. Correct. Both 'woman' and 'her' are accusative.
10. Correct. 'Him' and 'soldier' are both accusative.

Case

Here are two instances of difficulties in the use of the correct case of nouns and pronouns:

The case of words used as complements and in apposition

Case with compound subjects.

CASE WITH APPOSITION AND COMPLEMENTS

The rule is simple. Words used in apposition or as complements to nouns or pronouns take the same case as their antecedents.

Consider these sentences.

Exercise 100

1. We hurried to welcome our father, he who we honoured and respected so much.
2. The young woman, her to whom we sent the flowers, sent us a note of thanks.
3. It is funny to see a tourist, and he a teacher as well, fumbling for words, phrase-book in hand.
4. We went over to greet our cousins, they whom we had not seen for several years.
5. We were taken to see our teacher, she who the car had knocked down in the high street.
6. When the producer asked who was playing Juliet, I stood up and answered, 'It's me!'
7. Whom would you rather have been in a past life, Caesar or Antony?

8. That's him over there, the one with the scar.
9. Mrs Strong is in the kitchen, if it's her you want.
10. It's them you'd better speak to about the broken window.

Comment

1. . . . our father, **him whom** we honoured . . .
   accusative, in apposition to 'father', object of 'to welcome'.
2. The young woman, **she** to whom . . .
   nominative, in apposition to 'woman'.
3. . . . and **him** a teacher as well . . .
   accusative, in apposition to 'tourist'.
4. . . . our cousins, **them** whom we had not seen . . .
   accusative, in apposition to 'cousins'.
5. . . . teacher, **her** whom the car had . . .
   accusative in apposition to 'teacher'.
6. 'It's me' can stand. It is an accepted colloquialism and any correction would sound pedantic.
7. **Who** would you rather have been . . .
   nominative, complement to Caesar or Antony.
8. 'That's him' can stand. As in no. 6, any correction would sound unacceptable. ('That's he')
9. . . . if it's **she** you want . . .
   nominative, complement to 'it'. The expanded sentence would be: 'if it is she whom you want'.
10. 'It's they' is correct English; the other is colloquial.
    The awkwardness can be avoided by rephrasing the sentence.

Exercise 101

1. I shall give a special prize to he who wins three events on Sports Day.

2. Mr Jones said he would not waste time looking for they who had left the group and wandered off.
3. Mr Justice Clark did not think much of she who had left the baby to fend for itself at so tender an age.
4. This was a matter that was not going to be ignored by we who had worked so hard to put it right in the first place.
5. The decision was not going to help I who had claimed a grant for essential repairs.

Comment
1. . . . prize to **him** who . . .
2. . . . looking for **them** who had . . .
3. . . . think much of **her** who had left . . .
4. . . . ignored by **us** who had worked . . .
5. . . . going to help **me** who had claimed . . .

CASE WITH COMPOUND SUBJECTS

Exercise 102
Consider these sentences.

1. Me and my friends often go fishing.
2. The other players and me were made very welcome by the captain of the rival team.
3. Really, there is no difference between us and they.
4. Sally and he felt very important sitting up in a box with the Director.
5. My friend and her were overjoyed to see the dancers getting ready for the ballet performance.

Comment
1. Colloquially, this will do. Better, 'My friends and I . . .'

2. 'The other players and **I** . . .' 'I' is **nominative** as subject.

3. '. . . between us and **them**.' 'Between', a preposition, must be followed by an **accusative** case.

4. Correct. Sally and 'he' are both **nominative**, as subjects.

5. 'her' must be **'she'**, **nominative** subject of 'were overjoyed'. Better would be 'She and my friend . . .'

Ellipsis

The omission of words that should not be left out is an all-too-common feature of written English, for English is a language that readily leaves out words which can be omitted without damaging meaning.

OMISSION OF THE VERB

When two subjects occur with different requirements for agreement in number or person, a verb may be omitted.

Exercise 103
Consider these sentences.

1. John was rewarded for his bravery and his friends congratulated.
2. I am completely lost but Alice safe.
3. Three buses have gone by but the tram, at last, stopped.
4. London had been cleaned up but Sheffield, Newcastle and Liverpool left untouched.
5. The three other climbers have gone down at last but Old Rafferty not yet started to descend.
6. You are looking very smart but not your husband.
7. The yachtsmen were just rounding the top of the island but Peter Johnson only reached the first buoy.
8. Molly is having spaghetti but the boys hamburgers.

9. Running and walking are good for your circulation but sitting about not so good.
10. We are looking forward to an active holiday but lazy Jim only to reading and sleeping.

Comment

Fowler points out that this minefield is a large one. There is an English tradition of ellipsis – leaving out words which do not obscure meaning even if they dent the grammatical symmetry. This is specially so in speech, and a distinction has to be made between what we say and what we write. Standard written English will not countenance slovenly expression.

Here the issue is that subject and verb must agree in all respects.

1. . . . his friends **were** congratulated.   (number)
2. . . . Alice **is** safe.   (person)
3. . . . the tram **has** stopped.   (number)
4. . . . Liverpool **have been** left . . .   (number)
5. . . . Rafferty **has** not yet . . .   (number)
6. . . . but your husband **is** not.   (person)
7. . . . Peter Johnson **had** only . . .   (number)
8. . . . boys **are having** hamburgers.   (number)
9. . . . sitting about **is** not so.   (number)
10. . . . lazy Jim **is** only looking forward to . . .   (number)

OMISSION OF 'THAT' AS CONJUNCTION

Exercise 104
Consider these sentences.

1. The master was glad to see two boys had remembered that they were to visit a pickled onion factory.
2. It was my opinion he should have paid for his own ticket.
3. Jack Batty decided his team would kick off.
4. The French government declared they were not interested in N. Africa.
5. The sheepdog trial judge thought that he was right when he announced there would be no competition next year.
6. It is my view the RAF is not sufficiently equipped to do its job.
7. The referee declared the match was cancelled in view of the rain.
8. I noticed the MP for Bath asserted several times he was in favour of the Bill.
9. The solicitor gave it as his opinion the two women should be acquitted of the charge.
10. The child blurted out that he had been afraid to say who had taken the sweets because he was afraid he would be beaten up.

Comment
The following hints may prove useful.

A. Verbs that prefer **that** expressed:
   agree, assent, assume, calculate, conceive, hold, learn, maintain, reckon, remember, state, suggest.
B. Verbs that prefer **that** omitted:
   believe, presume, suppose, think.
C. Verbs where **that** can be expressed or omitted:
   be told, confess, consider, declare, grant, hear, know, propose, say, see, understand.

Thus:

> I agree **that** you should play tomorrow.
> I suppose you should play tomorrow.
> I know **that** you should play tomorrow.
> I know you should play tomorrow.

The inclusion of **that** in C. depends on the *tone*. **That** lends some dignity to the expression, whereas its omission tends to make the statement more colloquial.

> The shopkeeper understood **that** the rent would have to be raised.
> The shopkeeper understood the man did not know what he wanted.

Therefore . . .

1. . . . to see **that** two boys had remembered **that** they were . . .
2. . . . my opinion **that** he should have . . .
3. . . . decided **that** his team . . . (optional)
4. Omit 'that'.
5. . . . thought he was (omit 'that') . . . he announced **that** there would be . . .
6. . . . my view **that** the RAF . . .
7. Omit 'that'.
8. . . . several times **that** he was in favour . . .
9. . . . as his opinion **that** the two women . . .
10. . . . he was afraid he would be beaten up (omit 'that').

OMISSION AFTER 'THAN'

Exercise 105
Consider these sentences.

1. The results of the summer examinations were much less satisfactory than last year.
2. My neighbour's sunflowers have grown to a much greater height than mine.
3. The decision of the planning committee was more important to the builder than he could remember in his previous appeals.
4. The disappointing trade figures were less significant than previous months.
5. Greater respect for mother and father no man could claim to have.

Comment

An omission after **than** is common, and the rules are elusive. You have to balance the advantages of brevity against the need to ensure clarity of meaning and the logical sequence of ideas. These examples may help.

1. . . . satisfactory **than they were** last year . . .
2. . . . **than** the height mine have reached (or) . . . much higher than mine.
3. . . . **than** the importance of others he could remember (or) . . . than any other he could remember.
4. . . . **than** they had been in previous months.
5. . . . Begin: 'Greater respect **than that** he showed for mother and father . . .' The inversion here adds to the difficulty.

OMISSION OF PART OF A COMPOUND VERB

Exercise 106
Consider these sentences.

1. No country has or shall agree to the terms of that objectionable treaty.
2. Tom said the group neither would nor had they ever submitted to such unfair treatment.
3. We ought, in fact, we always have contributed to that charity.
4. You have or you certainly should ask for your money back on that loaf of bread.
5. The steamer is supposed and probably will dock at eight o'clock tonight.

Comment

The defective verb formations are obvious but, nevertheless, common.

1. No country has **agreed** or shall agree . . .
2. . . . neither would **submit** nor had they ever submitted . . .
3. We ought to **contribute**, in fact we always have contributed . . .
4. You have **asked** or you certainly should ask . . .
5. Rewrite: The steamer is supposed to dock at eight o'clock tonight and probably will do so.

Misuse of Negatives

Confusion arises occasionally, when negatives are used, as to just how far their powers of negation extend. Our interests here are:

Confusion of subject and verb.
Correct usage with 'neither'.
Pitfalls with the use of 'no'.
Uses of 'nor'.

CONFUSION OF SUBJECT AND VERB

Exercise 107
Consider these sentences.

1. No parcels must be kept for distribution on the next day but must be cleared as soon as they are received.
2. Few of the workmen were paid but were loyal enough to continue serving the firm out of gratitude for previous generosity.
3. I would not be surprised that spending so much time talking to her friends Joan did not miss her train.
4. It is not expected that candidates will answer all questions but will attempt at least five.
5. It is not thought that the train will be full and should have sufficient room for the school party.
6. Not a bit undismayed by the tragedy that occurred the previous evening, the planter went back into the forest.

7. It is unbelievable that if the car had been travelling so slowly that the accident would not have happened.
8. It would not be surprising if, by waiting too long in the rain, Sam had not caught a very bad cold.

Comment
Confusion is very common, and double negatives can be insidious.

1. No parcels must be cleared? Say . . . but **all** must be cleared.
2. Few were loyal enough? Say . . . but **all** were loyal . . .
3. . . . Joan missed her train.
4. It is expected that the candidates will **not** answer . . .
5. It is thought . . . will **not** be full . . .
6. Not a bit **dismayed** . . .
7. . . . the accident **would have** happened.
8. . . . in the rain, Sam **caught** a very bad cold.

CORRECT USAGE WITH 'NEITHER'

Exercise 108
Consider these sentences.

1. The accused was guilty of two crimes, neither of which are very serious.
2. What happened last night neither Tom nor Mary know.
3. Neither water nor petrol are able to clear off that stain.
4. Neither Mr Smith nor I is coming to the party tomorrow.

5. There is a new law which neither allows renting property nor selling it.
6. Their new dog is neither a pedigree boxer nor is he a bull-terrier.
7. Neither my cousin will be coming to the wedding, nor can the ceremony start before three o'clock.
8. Today we had something for lunch which was neither meat nor had it been fished out of the sea.
9. The book was neither a novel or a biography.
10. Neither John or Bill will be chosen as captain.

Comment

A. neither is **one** or **other** of **two**, so the following verb is the **singular** (nos 1–4).
B. Syntax demands that phrases and clauses after **neither** or **nor** are grammatically equivalent (nos 5–8).
C. **neither . . . or** is never right. Always use **neither . . . nor** (nos 9–10).

Thus

1. . . . neither of which **is** very serious.
2. . . . neither Tom nor Mary **knows**.
3. . . . neither water nor petrol **is** able . . .
4. Rewording necessary: I am not coming to the party tomorrow, nor is Mr Smith. (Neither Mr Smith nor I is? am).
5. . . . which allows **neither** renting **nor** selling property.
6. . . . is **neither** a pedigree boxer **nor** a bull-terrier.
7. Reword: My cousin will not be coming to the wedding, nor . . .
8. . . . which was certainly **not** meat **nor** . . .

9. . . . a novel **nor** a biography.
10. **neither** John **nor** Bill . . .

PITFALLS WITH THE USE OF 'NO'

Exercise 109
Consider these sentences.

1. Sheila, I fear, is a no suitable friend for our daughter.
2. Lord Blank amassed a no small fortune by selling refrigerators to Eskimos.
3. He will, under no circumstances, show you the files on our latest invention.
4. The refugees, in no conceivable way, will be able to reach the safety of a neutral country.
5. The electricians were reminded that, no more than any other group, were they entitled to a pay rise.
6. The doctor did not seem to understand, or not to appreciate, the gravity of the illness.
7. The umpire no-balled the bowler once again after he had already bowled three no balls.
8. No-body will leave the auditorium until the platform party has departed.
9. The caretaker checked that no one was left in the building.
10. Nowise was the superintendent going to give permission for the march to be held.

Comment
1. . . . is no suitable (or) . . . is not a suitable . . .
2. . . . amassed no small fortune . . .
3. Either: He will in no circumstances show
you . . . (no commas when using a

        parenthesis with 'no'), or

        He will not, in any circumstances, show . . .

4. Similarly: The refugees in no conceivable way will . . . or

        The refugees will not, in any conceivable way, be able . . .

5. Sentence is correct, **no** is an adverb.

6. Be careful of parallel constructions. Should read: . . . to understand, nor to appreciate . . .

7. Correct. As a verb: 'To no-ball'. As a noun: 'a no ball'.

8. **Nobody** should always be written thus.

9. **No one** is to be preferred.

10. **Nowise** as one word is correct, but write **in no wise** separately.

USES OF 'NOR'

Exercise 110
Consider these sentences.

1. The store detective said no one should be prosecuted or any other action taken about the thefts.

2. In spite of her wealth she had neither been to see us, or even sent us a card.

3. The shop had no oranges left, or could even get any from its depot.

4. The firemen did nothing to prevent the fire from spreading or even to help the victims to safety.

5. There was no hope of either stopping the train or of making the guard understand how ill Tommy was.

6. Because his uncle had not arrived, nor either of the two ladies who were supposed to come with

him, nor their luggage, which had been sent on in advance, we could do nothing but wait.

Comment

1. . . . be prosecuted **nor** any other action . . .
2. . . . been to see us **nor** even sent . . .
3. . . . oranges left, **nor** could it even . . .
4. Sentence correct.
5. Sentence correct.
6. Sentence correct. In these three last sentences the negatives 'nothing', 'no', 'not' and the 'nors' are correctly used.

Mistakes with Singular and Plural

CONFUSION WITH COLLECTIVES

Exercise 111
Consider these sentences.

1. The British government announces that they will defend Gibraltar.
2. Everyone must take their coat home tonight.
3. A herd of cows was crossing the road when a car ran into their rear.
4. Salaries will have to be improved if the number of doctors in hospitals are to be increased.
5. The Publishers' Guild hopes to issue their new brochure in March.
6. At last the committee has agreed to sanction the repairs, for which they have allocated £10,000.
7. The computer company, with the results of last year's trading before them, has agreed to increase prices by 5 per cent.
8. A crowd of youths surrounds the building, but the police are making sure they do not get inside.
9. The yacht squadron is leaving harbour and look as though they are beginning to deploy their ships across the Mediterranean.
10. Lord Grant's family have arrived at the Manor and is now settling in for the summer season.

Comment
Confusion arises because of the dual nature of collective nouns. They can be regarded as one group, hence

singular, or several people or things, and thus **plural**. Mistakes arise from mixing the two senses in the same context. In the sentences above, the collective nouns are given both identities, singular and plural, which offends both grammar and logic. We shall regard them in the singular sense.

1. . . . **it** will defend . . .
2. Everyone must take **his** or **her** coat home tonight.
   (The 'his/her' construction is not popular. 'His' at one time served both genders in a neutral way, but in these more sensitive times it is less acceptable. The matter can be resolved by changing the sentence: 'All of you must take your coats home'. 'Everyone', however, is singular and must always be regarded as such.)
3. . . . ran into **its** rear (or 'A herd of cows **were** crossing . . .')
4. . . . **is** to be increased.
5. . . . to issue **its** new brochure . . .
6. . . . **it has** allocated . . .
7. . . . trading before **it**, has agreed . . .
8. Better: 'A crowd of youths **surround** the building . . .'
9. . . . and **looks** as though **it** is beginning to deploy **its** ships . . .
10. . . . family **has** arrived . . .

'EACH' IS A SINGULAR WORD

Exercise 112
Consider these sentences.

1. Each of the waiters have three tables to look after.

2. Each player in the team must ensure that their kit is clean for Saturday.
3. They are each of them a Captain of Industry.
4. We each have our own personal badges for identification purposes.
5. The artists are famous each in their own way for painting and drawing.
6. Soon we shall be driving each of us our own car.
7. Each of the new electric cookers have a double oven.
8. Mary and Elizabeth each have their own bicycle now.
9. I bought a set of shelves and they each of them contain room for a dozen books.
10. Each of the dancers have many pairs of ballet shoes to change into.

Comment

'Each' is always **singular**.

1. . . . **has** three tables . . .
2. . . . that **his** (or **her**) kit is clean . . .
3. The sentence would be better written: Each of them **is** a Captain of Industry.
   When 'each' is not the subject, but in apposition with a plural subject, the verb and complement is also plural.
4. Similarly, sentence is correct.
5. Sentence correct.
6. . . . each of us **his** (or **her**) own car.
7. . . . **has** a double oven.
8. Sentence correct.
9. Sentence correct.
10. . . . **has** many pairs of shoes . . .

THE USES OF 'ONE'

Exercise 113

1. One is often asked whether they accept one-man-one-vote as a basis for democracy.
2. One is never satisfied with their job until one leaves it.
3. She is one of the best musicians who has played in the orchestra.
4. John Gielgud is notable as one of the best actors to play in Shakespearean roles.
5. The car was one of the fastest models that Ford has ever produced.
6. Sam was one of those lazy people who, whatever the circumstances, finds an excuse for dodging work.
7. Don Bradman was one of the greatest batting giants who have ever played in Test cricket.
8. 'Cats' is really one of the best musicals that has been produced on the London stage.
9. The man told everyone to leave their glasses on the table.
10. No one in their right mind would cross such a busy road without looking first.

Comment

1. . . . whether **he accepts** . . . (We can eschew the 'he' or 'she' refinement unless there is a specific requirement to make such distinction.)
2. . . . with **his** job . . .
3. . . . who **have** . . . (musicians, the antecedent, is plural).
4. Sentence correct.
5. Sentence correct.
6. . . . **find** an excuse . . .
7. Sentence correct.

8. . . . that **have** been produced . . .
9. . . . to leave **his** glass (**or rewrite the sentence**).
10. . . . in **his** right mind . . .

NUMBER CONFUSION AND THE USE OF THE COMPLEMENT

Exercise 114
1. The book's best feature are the illustrations.
2. A man dressed as a chimpanzee and a real chimpanzee is the same thing as far as appearances go.
3. The thing that is typically French are the wines and cheeses they produce.
4. The only hardship they suffered were the constant attacks by the rogue natives.
5. The most horrible event for Germany, and the one which eventually brought about her defeat, were the onslaughts of the Russian army.

Comment
Where subjects and complements differ in number, the verb should normally take the number of the subject.

1. . . . best feature **is** . . .
2. . . . **are** the same thing . . .
3. The thing . . . **is** the wines . . .
4. The only hardship . . . **was** . . .
5. The most horrible event . . . **was** . . .

NUMBER AFTER 'WHAT'

Exercise 115
1. What really interests the voters are the new

policies on the environment that the parties are putting out.

2. What is needed are a lot more doctors who are involved in community health.

3. What seems very important at this time, and what people say they want, are new guidelines on food hygiene.

4. What amazes my friends are the number of different activities that I can still undertake at the age of eighty.

5. What impresses the tourist in England are the constant changes of weather that we have to endure.

6. I am not sure what is the next steps that have to be taken in this matter.

7. The Board decided for what was apparently hardly valid reasons to dispense with Johnson's services.

8. The accountant drew attention to what was referred to as concealed and false entries in the ledger books.

9. They disagreed with what was, in their opinion, unnecessary criticisms of the employees' conduct.

10. His health recovered after what appears to have been many successful operations on his heart.

Comment

'What' can be singular (= 'that which', a 'thing') or it can be plural, where its meaning does not depend on any complement. A clear head and courage will see you through!

1. . . . the voters **is** . . .
2. What is needed **is** a lot more . . .
3. . . . they want, **is** . . .

4. What amazes my friends **is** . . .
5. . . . in England **is** . . .
6. . . . what **are** the next steps . . .
7. . . . what **were** apparently . . .
8. . . . to what **were** referred to . . .
9. . . . with what **were**, in their opinion . . .
10. . . . after what **appear** to have been . . .

SINGULAR OR PLURAL SUBJECTS AND PLURAL OR SINGULAR VERBS

Exercise 116

1. A great deal of fuss and bother are caused by traffic jams these days.
2. The shopkeeper showed him several different knives, the sharpness of which were quite frightening.
3. John's sharing out of the hundreds of dear departed Uncle Harry's photographs were a delight to all the younger members of the family.
4. I gave Mary a small amount of Italian coins which are still valid in that country.
5. The special measures the government has now taken to combat inflation seems to have been ineffective.
6. Schubert's set of Impromptus, one of his greatest piano works, still find many admirers among today's audiences.
7. The de luxe editions of the *Encyclopaedia Britannica*, in its leather binding, sells for just under £2,000.
8. The Americans have banned the export of those pesticides whose use in other countries have proved harmful to everyone.
9. If the sender or postal clerk are to blame for non-

delivery, one of them must pay.
10. As the birth will be difficult, either the mare or the foal are to die, I am afraid.

Comment
1. A great deal . . . **is** caused . . .
2. . . . the sharpness of which **was** quite frightening.
3. John's sharing out . . . **was** a delight . . .
4. Sentence is correct.
5. The special measures . . . **seem** to . . .
6. Schubert's set . . . still **finds** . . .
7. The de luxe **edition** . . . sells for . . .
8. . . . whose use . . . **has** proved . . .
9. . . . **is** to blame . . .
10. either the mare or the foal **is** to die . . .

CONFUSION WITH SINGULAR OR PLURAL SUBJECTS

Exercise 117
1. Eventually there was inserted in the Treaty of Versailles by the victorious allies several guilt clauses which later proved an intolerable problem.
2. The Authority established a class of disruptive and unruly pupils, extracted from a number of surrounding schools, which were soon to be the cause of a national scandal.
3. When the Round-the-World sailing race gets under way there is likely to be several accidents, some of which may prove serious.
4. This was once a peaceful village where now stands an extensive parking plot, supermarket stores and even two pleasure parks.

5. The twins have many natural charms, and to these are now added a vast fortune, left to them by an eccentric millionaire.

Comment

1. . . . there **were** inserted . . . (clauses)
2. . . . which **was** soon . . . (a class)
3. . . . there **are** likely to be . . . (accidents)
4. . . . where now **stand** . . . (plural subject follows)
5. . . . to these **is** now added . . . (fortune)

Participles and Gerunds

UNATTACHED PARTICIPLES

Exercise 118

1. Not having received your cheque in payment, you may now expect a letter from our solicitors.
2. Seven candidates failed to complete the paper not counting the two who were taken ill.
3. Granting that it might rain, the coach will still leave at eight a.m.
4. Speaking of clothes, Harrods has just received some exclusive coats from Paris.
5. The roses have opened beautifully, even allowing for the lack of sunshine.
6. Worked out on the basis of one teacher to every twenty pupils, the school will need twenty-seven teachers.
7. The judge sentenced the prisoner to three years' imprisonment, having been caught with the silver in the back of his car.
8. Knowing that the train would be late, the refreshment room stayed open until ten o'clock.
9. Considering the poor acoustics of the concert hall, the soprano sang beautifully.
10. Proving themselves the worst English team in twenty years, the Australians won the series five matches to nil.

Comment

The present and past participles in these sentences, because they are adjectives, need to attach themselves to a noun, here the subject of the sentence. When one does this, the absurdity of the statements becomes obvious. Thus:

1. As **you** have not received your cheque . . .
2. **The seven candidates** were not counting the two . . .
3. **The coach** granted that it might rain . . .
4. **Harrods** was speaking of clothes . . .

Correct by turning the participle phrase into a clause or by rejigging the main clause:

1. As **we** have not received your cheque . . . (or) . . . your cheque in payment, **we** shall be sending you a solicitor's letter.
2. Seven candidates, not counting . . . failed . . .
3. **Even** if it rains the coach will still leave . . .
4. Speaking of clothes, **I can tell you that** Harrods . . .
5. . . . have opened beautifully, even **when one allows** . . .
6. **If one takes as a basis** one teacher for every twenty pupils, the school will need . . .
7. . . . sentenced the prisoner **who had been caught** with the silver in the back of his car to three . . .
8. . . . would be late, **the manageress kept** the refreshment room open . . .
9. **In spite of** the poor acoustics . . .
10. **As the English fielded** the worst team in . . .

UNPOSSESSED GERUNDS

Exercise 119

1. John coming home late at night made his mother very anxious.

2. The constable did not approve of the tramp pretending he was a respectable citizen.
3. Watch young Peter, check every morning on him washing himself.
4. Mary walking home by herself could be very dangerous.
5. The government pretending that it is not responsible is really quite unacceptable.
6. Jenny was looking forward to us arriving from New York after all that time.
7. Mr Parker painting the front of our house was a disaster we shall never forget.
8. Poor Betty could not endure the baby crying all night long.
9. The man claiming to be the victim of an assault is nothing but a transparent lie.
10. The producer did not like them singing so loudly in the first chorus of the scene.

Comment

In these sentences the verbal idea expressed in the gerunds (-ing) requires an agent to complete its meaning: **whose** coming home? **whose** pretending? **whose** washing? It follows that the agent needs to *possess* the action denoted, and must wear the appropriate grammatical clothing to show his possession, i.e. an apostrophe.

1. **John's** coming home . . .
2. . . . the **tramp's** pretending . . .
3. . . . on **his** washing himself.
4. **Mary's** walking home . . .
5. The **government's** pretending . . .
6. . . . to **our** arriving . . .
7. **Mr Parker's** painting . . .
8. . . . **the baby's** crying . . .

9. **The man's** claiming . . .
10. . . . did not like **their** singing . . .

There may be occasions when a strict application of the rules seems to break down. Consider:

I could hear Jim rustling the sweet papers during the opera. Are we going to say '**Jim's** rustling the sweet papers'? I don't think so. It can be said that 'Jim' is the person I can hear, and 'rustling' can legitimately be considered a participle, a kind of adjective, and we have a 'rustling-the-sweet-papers' Jim. Similarly:

Yesterday we noticed Mrs Robinson entertaining her relatives from Australia.
It is '**Mrs Robinson**', we notice. What kind of 'Mrs Robinson'?
An 'entertaining-her-relatives-from-Australia' Mrs Robinson.

And again:

The policeman wanted to stop the children buying cigarettes.
(Not 'the **children's** buying')

The woman watched him lighting the bonfire.
(Not 'his lighting the bonfire')

Instead of Harry sending a message to headquarters . . .
(Not 'Harry's sending a message')

But

I don't like **your** spending all that money on clothes.
(It's the 'spending' I don't like, not 'you')

He protested against **the Bishop of Gloucester's**
holding a service . . .
(It's the 'holding of the service' that he protests
against, not specifically the Bishop)

GERUNDS AND INFINITIVES

Exercise 120
1. I look forward to see Charles tomorrow.
2. He objects to wait for an hour for a bus.
3. The Council agrees in committee to allow
development along the riverside.
4. The police were concerned at the habit of a
number of motorists to park on the yellow lines.
5. Mother's plan to cook everything the day before
went all wrong.
6. His neighbours claimed that he had no intention
to build a fence round the yew tree.
7. John had no intention to discuss his promotion
prospects with his boss.
8. The gardener had the satisfaction to see all his
roses bloom that year.
9. The milkman felt he had a duty to deliver his
orders even though the snow was almost impass-
able.
10. His friend took upon himself the duty to see that
Mr Murphy had a daily walk every morning.

Comment
The question is: Does one use the gerund ('to . . .'
form) or the participle ('-ing') form after certain verbs?

'I look forward to see Charles tomorrow', OR
'I look forward to seeing Charles tomorrow'?

This is not so much a matter of grammar as of idiom. In general, the participle is less offensive than the gerund. Fowler suggests we are led to the gerund (the infinitive) by *analogy*, by words that are sufficiently close to other words where the infinitive is a legitimate choice. Examples may help:

1. to **seeing** him
2. to **waiting**
3. to allow (correct)
4. **of parking**
5. **of cooking**
6. **of building**
7. **of discussing**
8. **of seeing**
9. to deliver (correct)
10. duty to see (correct)

Students may refer to the *Primer* (p. 58) for a list of the correct prepositions to follow verbs, but the instances are so numerous that a full list is not possible.

Position of Adverbs

Care must be taken to ensure that **adverbs** and **adverbial phrases** are correctly (i.e. logically) placed in sentences. In this section we shall discuss:

The split infinitive.
Adverbs used with compound verbs.
Adverbs separating verb and object.
The position of 'only'.
The position of 'however'.
The position of 'therefore'.

THE SPLIT INFINITIVE

Exercise 121 (and see Exercise 51)
Consider these sentences.

1. George reviewed the progress he had made and resolved to now concentrate all his efforts on revision.
2. Penny was now going to elegantly dance her way into the front line of the ballet.
3. In view of the economic crisis the Chancellor had to seriously consider raising taxes.
4. Because the guilty man had no job, the Court ordered the plaintiff to at least allow him time to pay off the debt.
5. Seven more months to finally achieve his goal did not seem long to the ambitious mountaineer.
6. I believe the doctors are too incompetent to correctly diagnose complaints of that nature.

7. The professor did not want the chemicals to completely be covered by water.
8. The new intake of students is to be gradually initiated into college routine.
9. That new chapter needs to be thoroughly understood before we can move on.
10. The aircraft are to be fully dispersed around the airfield in case we are bombed by the enemy.

Comment

Few flags in English grammar are flown so bravely as that of the **split infinitive**, and few war cries bring out the backwoodsmen with such speed. The general rule advocated here was stated in the *Primer* (p. 79): infinitives should not be split. Two things need to be said. First, accusations of infinitive splitting are sometimes levelled at examples that are patently innocent; a word about these later. Second, some bold writers, sure of their competence, occasionally hoist a 'manifesto of independence' and should be acknowledged for their courage and, not infrequently, their rightness. As for the sentences above:

1. . . . and now resolved to concentrate . . . (inelegant and wrong)
2. . . . was going to dance her way elegantly into . . . (clumsy)
3. A . . . seriously had to consider . . . (awkward)
   B . . . had seriously to consider . . . (awkward)
   C . . . Retain the split infinitive? Possibly. Perhaps here we have a new infinitive: **to seriously consider**, a more emphatic form of its parent and valid in its own right.
4. . . . the plaintiff at least to allow him time . . .
5. Either retain as it is (see 3C above) or omit 'finally'.

6. . . . to diagnose correctly complaints . . .
7. . . . to be completely covered . . .
8. Sentence correct.
9. Sentence correct.
10. A third example of correct usage.

Note: 'To be covered', 'initiated', 'understood', 'dispersed' are present infinitives passive, but no damage is done by inserting an adverb after 'to be'. The flow of words is natural, and objections to this practice are only obstructive.

ADVERBS USED WITH COMPOUND VERBS

Exercise 122
1. If his evidence eventually is admitted, the jury must find him guilty.
2. Our standard of cleanliness generally will ensure the safety of all staff.
3. The English team certainly are preparing for the new series of matches in Europe.
4. Without international aid, the children undoubtedly will suffer from famine this winter.
5. The popular TV star also was engaged in two West End shows for the pantomime season.

Comment
The following order is to be preferred, where the adverb comes between the two parts of the verb.

1. . . . is eventually . . .
2. . . . will generally . . .
3. . . . are certainly . . .
4. . . . will undoubtedly . . .
5. . . . was also engaged . . .

ADVERBS SEPARATING VERB AND OBJECT

Exercise 123

1. I shall be considering during the coming week your request for leave of absence.
2. The lashing rain prevented for a time any further play.
3. The judges decided for many reasons to award no prize that year.
4. Professor Potts delivered with much humour and erudition his lecture entitled 'Whether elephants go to sleep standing up'.
5. The merchant sold at a handsome profit all the goods on his stall.
6. The chairman and chief executive were promoting their arguments very persuasively for taking over the rival company on the Continent.
7. The Captain issued yesterday several orders to his officers for the next day's manoeuvres.
8. The boss dismissed without warning a number of workers who protested against the cuts in hours.

Comment

Adverbs, or adverbial phrases, should not, as a general rule, come between a transitive verb and its object. Their proper position is either before or after a verb.

1. . . . considering, during the coming week, you request . . . (Commas are the best solution here, otherwise 'leave of absence during the coming week' could be inferred).
2. Perhaps begin with 'For a time . . .'
3. Again begin with the phrase, 'For many reasons . . .'

4. Consign 'with much humour and erudition' to the end of the sentence.
5. 'at a handsome profit' to the end of the sentence.
6. 'very persuasively' to the end.
7. Begin with 'Yesterday . . .'
8. The best position for 'without warning' is at the beginning of the sentence. To place it after 'workers' tends to isolate the relative 'who'.

THE POSITION OF 'ONLY'

Exercise 124
1. He only died last Wednesday.
2. Johnson only had difficulties with the drop kick, at other times his accuracy is uncanny.
3. It could only be foolish to think of him as a hero because of his bravery at El Alamein.
4. Marmalade should only be served at breakfast.
5. Mrs Jackson only had to decide which pair of shoes to buy.
6. The Inter-City trains can only now be used for cheap fares at certain times of the day.
7. If only the cakes had not all been eaten, we could have enjoyed a nice tea.
8. I crossed the bridge only to get to my destination more quickly.
9. The committee decided they could only come to a proper conclusion if a survey of the area was undertaken first.
10. William only asked the question because he was interested in that kind of mathematical problem.

Comment
Many commentators have pointed out that, in a search for correct grammatical practice, we have not infre-

quently to strike a balance between pedantic correct-
ness and sensible, acceptable usage. The issue is: How
best to convey your meaning accurately. If what you
write ends in ambiguity or fuzziness, you should think
again. This applies to written material. In conversation and dialogue, usage is often more lax, and licence
is permitted that no grammarian would sanction for
the written word.

The word **only** is a case in point. Fowler gives the
example; 'He only died a week ago.' He chides the
pedants who would insist on 'He died only a week ago'
as those who would turn language into an exact science
or an automatic machine. Such a point of view merits
support. No one would misunderstand 'He only died a
week ago', and we waste valuable energy disputing
about this idiomatic usage when the word 'only'
offends much more seriously in other examples.

'Only' should be placed (usually) directly before or
(occasionally) directly after the word or phrase it
modifies.

A. Only *I* gave him three marks out of ten.
B. I only *gave* him three marks out of ten.
C. I gave only *him* three marks out of ten.
D. I gave him only *three* marks out of ten.
E. I gave him three marks out of ten *only*.

In the first four sentences the emphatic words are in
italics. A, C and D are explicit in meaning, the word
following 'only' is the important one. In E the
placement is clumsy, giving a meaning hardly disting-
uishable from D. B is the troublesome one. Logically
it has little justification. 'I only *gave* three marks . . .'
I did not sell them? or withdraw them? or fiddle them?
Its meaning is grammatically insecure and yet, to
convey meaning D, it would probably occur more

frequently. In colloquial usage, the word 'only' exerts a modifying influence over the whole sentence and might well be acceptable. A, B and D, however, are specific in meaning and illustrate how crucial the placement of this word in a sentence is.

Thus:

1. Acceptable.
2. . . . only with the drop kick . . .
3. . . . as a hero only because of . . .
4. . . . only at breakfast.
5. Acceptable. More pedantically . . . only which pair of shoes . . .
6. . . . only at certain times . . .
7. Acceptable.
8. Correct sentence.
9. . . . only if a survey . . .
10. . . . only because he was interested . . .

THE POSITION OF 'HOWEVER'

Exercise 125

1. Peter wondered however he survived in that icy sea.
2. No one could understand however the brave fireman endured the fierce heat.
3. I wondered however I could repay my parents for their kindness.
4. However he reached home that night will always be a puzzle to me.
5. Mary asked however she was supposed to wash all those dishes by herself.
6. I asked to see the manager. He, however, was busy and could not spare the time.

7. The room was crowded. Mary, however, made her way to the door and slipped out unnoticed.
8. It was an extraordinarily dark night. Jim, however, strode through the wood and kept searching for the missing child.

Comment

In conversation, **how ever** is used as an emphatic form of *how*? It should not be used in writing. When **how** is combined with **ever**, in that word's separate sense of 'at any time', it should then be parted from it by some other word or words. To combine them is wrong, often compounded by printing them as one word. Thus:

1. . . . **how** he **ever** survived . . .
2. . . . **how** the brave firemen **ever** endured . . .
3. . . . **how** I could **ever** repay . . .
4. **How** he **ever** reached home . . .
5. Mary asked **how** she was **ever** supposed to wash . . . or omit 'ever'.

When **however** is used purely for emphasis, its position is crucial. Placed second in a sentence, it draws attention to the first word and you should decide if that is what you intend.

6. What is probably meant is:
   . . . the manager. However, he was busy . . .
7. . . . However, Mary made her way . . .
8. . . . However, Jim strode through . . .

Note: **But** together with **however** is superfluous.

But I must point out, however, that the matter cannot be discussed today . . .
But your ideas, however, are not supported by any evidence . . .

Either **but** or **however**, but never both. Thus:

However, I must point out . . .
But your ideas are not supported . . .

THE POSITION OF 'THEREFORE'

Exercise 126
1. He cannot be home as early as that and, therefore, we must find someone else.
2. The dog has not been for his walk yet therefore you must take him as soon as you have changed.
3. She has to play the part of a queen; her dress, therefore, must be regal and resplendent.
4. The House of Commons voted against capital punishment, therefore, the Bill did not go to the Lords.
5. This by-law affects us greatly; we, therefore, shall have to consult our solicitors for guidance.

Comment
The placing of a comma before **therefore** throws emphasis on the preceding word. Where such emphasis is not required, the comma should not be used.

The position of **therefore** is also important. As with **however**, when placed second in the sentence, it puts the emphasis on the first word and you must decide if this is what you want.

1. Omit commas, since no emphasis for 'and' is required.
2. . . . yet, therefore . . . comma is needed simply to separate the two clauses.
3. Commas required. 'dress' is the important word.
4. Omit the comma after **therefore**.
5. Correct; emphasis is drawn to 'we'.

Relative Pronouns

When we notice that in this section we are dealing mainly with six very common, work-a-day words (*what, that, which, who, whom, whose*) and predominantly two grammatical functions (case, and defining and non-defining clauses), the complexity of some of the issues raised is remarkable. The misuse of these enabling words – which enable us to condense and vary our writing effectively and help us to achieve an easy fluency in referring back to previously stated ideas – is endemic in speech and only too frequently met in writing. Your responsibility is to equip yourself with knowledge of the grammatical foundations upon which the correct use of these words is built and to understand why right practices are right and wrong ones wrong.

The words have a chameleon-like character and because of this will be considered under these headings:

Defining and non-defining clauses.
'What'.
'That':   As adjective.
           As adverb.
           As conjunction.
           As relative adverb.
           Subject to double government.
'Which': Relative and demonstrative uses.
           Serving two verbs.
           . . . in *which* to . . .
           'Which'/'that'/'who'.
           After a superlative.
           As relative adverb.

'Which' and 'who' with collective nouns.
'Who':   and *that*.
          and *whom*.
'Whose'.
'Who ever' and 'whoever'.
'Than'.

Readers who notice a resemblance to the categories originally isolated by the brothers Fowler can congratulate themselves on their detective work. Their pioneering analysis of the problems with these words has not been bettered and it would be a poor tribute to them to have ignored their original and comprehensive studies. It is hoped that some overlapping will be excused, as it is difficult to avoid.

DEFINING AND NON-DEFINING CLAUSES

Exercise 127 (see *Primer*, pp. 15 ff.)
Insert commas where required in these sentences, and make any other necessary corrections.

1. The Rhine which runs through Germany is not a clean river.
2. The man that attacked me was arrested.
3. He that commits a murder must pay the penalty.
4. My 'Algebra for Beginners' that I left in the bus was returned by the garage.
5. The City of London which must be very wealthy gave a large donation to charity.
6. The building that stands on the corner of the High Street is to be pulled down soon.
7. Cleopatra's Needle which was brought here from Egypt stands on the Thames Embankment.

8. My homework which is always late landing on the teacher's desk was all wrong as usual.
9. Our unique Meissen statuette which father bought in Germany is reputed to be worth £6,000.
10. The opera that I like best is 'Der Rosenkavalier'.

Comment

A **defining** relative clause precisely identifies its antecedent.

A **non-defining** relative clause does not have to do this because the identity is already contained in the antecedent. Thus:

Defining (A):   The river *that flows from York to the coast* is always busy with small craft.

Non-defining (B): The River Dee, *which we passed on the way to Wales*, is very picturesque.

In (A), if we omit the relative clause we lose the identity of the river. In other words, the clause **defines** the particular river under discussion.

In (B), omission of the relative clause detracts nothing from the identity of the River Dee, which is already defined for us. The clause, therefore, is **non-defining**; it simply adds a further piece of information.

Rule 1. Non-defining clauses should be separated by a comma from their antecedents, with two commas if they are placed in parenthesis.

Rule 2. Use 'that' as the defining relative and 'which' (or 'who') as the non-defining relative.

But note some exceptions:

1. 'that' is not used of persons; 'who' is preferred.
2. 'which' is sometimes used to prevent the ending of a sentence with a preposition and
3. 'which' is used to avoid 'that that'.

Comments on Exercise 127

1. The Rhine, which runs through Germany, is . . . (non-defining)
2. Correct. (Or 'who attacked me') (defining)
3. Correct, but 'He who . . .' (defining)
4. . . . Beginners', which I left in the bus, was . . . (non-defining)
5. . . . London, which must be very wealthy, gave . . . (non-defining)
6. Correct. (defining)
7. . . . Needle, which was brought here from Egypt, stands . . . (non-defining)
8. My homework, which is always late . . . desk, was . . . (non-defining)
9. . . . statuette, which father bought in Germany, is . . . (non-defining)
10. Correct. (defining).

Exercise 128

1. John had seen many boxers in his time but not one he thought with a face like Walker's.
2. Peter who arrived only yesterday wanted to take over the entire running of the conference.
3. The new man surprised the Board by the ideas which he presented.
4. During the first race which was timed for 3.30 p.m. two horses fell at the river bend.
5. The Lord Harry who sent me this letter is not the same Lord Harry we met in Parliament Square.

6. Prefects will be chosen by the School Council which must gradually assume more responsibility for the conduct of school affairs.
7. The biggest fish I ever caught was the pike in the Lune.
8. My youngest son who was present all through the play thought it was very boring.
9. The two men from the Electricity Board whose names were Thomas and Peter did the job in no time.
10. The moon that circles round Neptune is apparently green in colour.

Comment

1. . . . but not one, he thought, with a . . . (non-defining)
2. Peter, who . . . yesterday, wanted to . . . (non-defining)
3. . . . by the ideas that he presented. (defining)
4. . . . race, which was timed for 3.30 p.m., two horses . . . (non-defining)
5. Correct. (defining)
6. . . . School Council, which must . . . (non-defining)
7. Correct. (defining)
8. My youngest son, who was . . . play, thought . . . (non-defining)
9. . . . Electricity Board, whose names were . . . Peter, (non-defining)
10. Correct. (defining).

'WHAT'

'What' and number

Exercise 129
Correct these sentences where necessary.

1. What is necessary are arrangements that are fair to everyone.
2. What I believe that recipe needs are lots of garlic and a pint of cream to make it more tasty.
3. What mystifies me is the crowds of people who will pay to see such rubbish.
4. What is important to watch are all the details of the legislation that are being discussed.
5. I agreed, for what was, in my opinion, the best reasons, to accept the Council's ruling.
6. The girls tried to decide what were the appropriate clothes to wear for the journey.
7. The soldiers agreed that what to them was the most dangerous aspects of the campaign should be tackled first.
8. The maid did not know what was, according to her mistress, the first jobs she had to do that morning.

Comment
A good general rule is that when 'what' begins its journey as a singular pronoun, the verbs dependent on it remain singular. However, 'what' can be plural and, again, consistency in number value should be respected. Hence:

1. What is necessary **is** arrangements . . .
2. . . . that recipe needs **is** lots of garlic . . .
3. Correct.

4. . . . important to watch **is** all the details . . . (the thing **is**)
5. . . . for what **were** . . . the best reasons . . .
6. Correct.
7. . . . what to them **were** the most dangerous aspects . . .
8. . . . what **were** . . . the first jobs she had . . .

Exercise 130

1. The man's action was wrong, but what I wish to say is that there are certain circumstances when he might have been right.
2. I know of no other player who has such skill to produce what appears to be, when he plays them, such master-strokes of batting.
3. Despite the outcry all over the world, what most people believe is required are regular meetings and more effort to supply the refugees with food.
4. Few actors have the power to portray what appears, when he plays them, to be lifelike characters that one might meet every day in the street.
5. What are needed are not small increases given to the workers each year, but a wholesale restructuring of scales that will give everyone a substantial increase in pay.

Comment

Sometimes 'what' requires us to find a noun not necessarily placed in the complement, but one of wider meaning or referring to the vaguer sense of 'what' to be found in **that which**. In the above sentences, the matter of number should be tackled along these lines:

1. Correct. The thing I wish to say **is** . . .
2. . . . to produce what **appear** to be . . .

To produce (the things) that **appear** to be . . .
3. . . . believe **are** required are regular meetings . . .
4. . . . to portray what **appear**, when he plays them, to be . . .
5. What **is** needed **is** not small increases . . .
(The thing or measure) that **is** needed **is** . . .

'WHAT' AND PREPOSITION CONFUSION

Exercise 131
1. What the Chairman was anxious in his report was to show that urgent steps had to be taken for the safety of the public.
2. What the Jenkins family hired for £10 a day last year they had to pay £20 this year when they went on holiday.
3. Facing the teacher with feelings very different from what he had faced him before Billy confessed he had played truant on the previous day.
4. I am not sure that I am getting what I want and for which I came all this way.
5. Jane was applauded when she came on stage in what was described as the 'in' dress of the year and for which the designer was asking £600.

Comment
1. The sentence is defective. It does not satisfy the dual nature of 'what' = **that which**. Rewrite as follows:
What the Chairman was anxious **to do** in his report was to show . . .
2. Rewrite: What the Jenkins family hired for £10 a day last year they had to pay £20 **for** this year . . .
3. . . . very different from what he had faced him **with** before . . .

4. . . . that I am getting what I want and come all this way for.

The original sentence has been constructed as a means of avoiding the dreaded preposition at the end of the sentence, quite needlessly.

5. (Correct, or) . . . what was described as the 'in' dress of the year and what the designer was asking £600 for.

'What' and case usage

Exercise 132
1. He pretends to know what the metal is and its parts consist of.
2. As for salary, I shall give him what he wants and the company thinks he ought to have.
3. Tell the class to concentrate on what they can do and is necessary to complete the assignment.
4. You will have to find out what the animal is and did to the man it attacked.
5. See if anyone can discover what he is doing now and makes him come back to this district.

Comment

The same word cannot serve the needs of two different case usages. If in one instance it is used as a nominative word and then subsequently as an accusative, it has to be repeated, even though there is no need in English, as there is in other languages, to change its form.

In the sentences above, 'what' as a single word has been asked to serve two masters, and this will not do. Additional 'whats' are needed.

1. . . . what the metal is and **what** its parts consist of.
2. The sentence is correct. 'What' is in the accusa-

tive case in both roles it plays: the object of 'give' and of 'the company thinks he ought to have'.

3. . . . what they can do and **what** is necessary to complete . . .

4. . . . what the animal is and **what it** did to the man . . .

5. . . . what he is doing now and **what** makes him come back . . .

'what' is the object of 'he is doing' and the subject of 'makes him come back'.

'THAT'

'That' as an adjective

Exercise 133

1. There is that honesty about the first applicant.
2. She was in that rush to get home.
3. My brother has that knowledge of French I hesitate to argue with him.
4. The children showed that interest we were in the museum for two hours.
5. The wind had that iciness about it, I nearly wept with the cold.
6. He has that fear of Smith that I believe he will never go near him again.

Comment

That is a perfectly acceptable demonstrative adjective ('I would like that book', 'Could I have that seat, please?'), but in the above examples its use, though formerly good English, is now colloquial only. Rewrite:

1. There is **an air of** honesty . . .
2. She was in **such a** rush . . .

3. My brother has **so much** knowledge . . .
4. . . . showed **so much** interest . . .
5. The wind had **such an intense** iciness . . .
6. He has **such a great** fear . . .

'That' as an adverb

Exercise 134
1. I am that hungry I could eat a horse.
2. The man is that worried, he might do himself an injury.
3. It's not that important.
4. The headmaster is that grumpy this morning, someone will suffer.
5. I did not know you were that interested in archaeology.
6. I am not that anxious to visit Aunt Kate.

Comment
This adverbial use of 'that' is acceptable, perhaps, only in speech when an actual demonstration is possible: e.g. David is that tall. Otherwise it is inadmissible.

Corrections can be supplied by using 'so' in most cases or by judiciously recasting the sentence.

Note: Care is needed in using 'that' with a participle or phrase:

1. *That section referring* to the United Nations charter was deleted from the report.
2. Their criticism was regarded with *that contempt usually reserved* for the scribblings of provincial reporters.
3. The Minister could give no suitable answer to *that question asked by* the Member for Derby.

In all such cases it is proper to put 'the' in place of 'that' in these extracts.

'That' as a conjunction

Exercise 135

1. The Captain warned us that unless we played well on Saturday night we would all be dropped from the team next week.
2. I must tell you that, had the pupils not done their homework, wouldn't they have been kept in after school.
3. My father said if we came home early let us all go out to the cinema.
4. The price of things increases so rapidly these days that who can tell where it will end.
5. The judge felt that if he passed a lenient sentence who would say how much more crime would be committed.

Comment

A subordinate clause introduced by 'that' must take the form of a statement, not a question or command. Hence:

1. . . . Saturday, we might all be dropped . . .
2. . . . homework, they would have been . . .
3. . . . early we could all go . . .
4. . . . that no one can tell . . .
5. . . . sentence, no one could say how much . . .

Functions of 'that' as a conjunction

1. Introduces a **noun clause** as **subject**:

That he is late is obvious to everyone.

That Russia wants peace is a position we have to accept.

2. Introduces a **noun clause** as **object**:

   I know *that you have been waiting.*
   He told me *that John was in hospital.*

3. Introduces an **adverbial clause**:

   The storm was so severe *that we had to take cover.*
   The animal is so large *that it must be kept in a cage.*

'That' as a relative adverb

Exercise 136

1. The committee cannot treat the ratepayers with the contempt that it treated the other petitioners.
2. The Tate Gallery found itself in the same position that the National Gallery had found itself after the cut-backs.
3. You cannot regard saving money for a holiday in the same light that we regard saving money for a house.
4. Hitler was in the same situation after Stalingrad that Napoleon found himself after Warsaw.
5. I advised against pleading guilty for the very reason that he had already received advice from his own family.
6. The sailors watched the overcast sky with all the anxiety that a young girl at her first dance surveys the regiment of young men in the ballroom.
7. The greatest danger on the motorways is the speed that cars tail each other in the fast lane.

8. The prisoner reached for the top bar of the fence that he pulled himself over and escaped.

Comment
In these sentences 'that' is used as 'which', plus a preposition.

1. . . . the contempt **with which** it treated . . .
2. . . . position **in which** the National Gallery . . .
3. . . . in the same light **in which** we regard . . .
4. . . . after Stalingrad **in which** Napoleon . . .
5. . . . the very reason **for which** he had . . .
6. . . . the anxiety **with which** a young girl . . .
7. . . . the speed **at which** cars . . .
8. . . . of the fence **by which** he pulled . . .

'That' subject to double government

Exercise 137
1. Charlotte Rousse is a dessert that I am very fond of and can be found in all good restaurants.
2. That is the throne on which Charles II was crowned and regarded always with great affection.
3. My son had a toy that he played with for a long time but finally was lost in the woods.
4. World War I brought about a political upheaval that troubled Europe for over twenty years and many countries used as an excuse for World War II.
5. I found his fiancée a girl that I disapproved of but was apparently acceptable to everyone else.
6. This is the table that he put his books on when he came in and left in a terrible mess.
7. I saw a hat that I liked and bought for Jane.

8. The flower was one that he had grown from seed, and won a prize at the local show.

Comment
When 'that' (or 'which') is repeated in a sentence, even if its repetition is merely 'understood', make sure that its government (i.e. case) is the same, otherwise the word itself must be repeated or another one substituted for it.

1. . . . of which (accusative) . . . . . . and **which** (nominative) can be found . . .
2. . . . crowned and **which he** regarded always . . .
3. . . . but finally **it** was lost . . .
4. . . . years, **one that** many countries used . . .
5. . . . disapproved of but **she** was apparently . . .
6. . . . came in and **which** he left . . .
7. Sentence correct. 'That' is object of both 'liked' and 'bought'.
8. . . . from seed, and **it** won a prize . . .

'WHICH'

Relative and demonstrative uses

Exercise 138
1. He took control of the boat, his steering of which leaving everyone gasping for breath.
2. The stewards were worried about the new racing cars, the drivers of which hurtling round the track at dangerous speeds.
3. She pointed out the beautiful park the seats of which stretching out into the distance where the stream ran.

4. They refused to fly the relief supplies in British planes by which means depriving the refugees of the supplies they needed.
5. He lost his train ticket for which reason reaching work late and being warned about time-keeping.

Comment

The relative must play two roles: refer back to its antecedent and lead on to attach itself to a subordinate clause. In the above sentences there seems to be confusion between the relative and a demonstrative 'this' or 'these', i.e. 'He took control of the boat'; this 'leaving everyone gasping for breath'. The sentences can be corrected in one of two ways, as indicated.

1. Either: . . . his steering of **it** . . . or . . . his steering of **which left** . . .
2. . . . the drivers of which **hurtled** . . . or . . . **with their drivers hurtling** . . .
3. . . . **stretched** out . . . or . . . **with its seats** stretching . . .
4. . . . by which means **they deprived** . . . or . . . **thus** depriving . . .
5. . . . **he reached work late** and **was** warned . . . or . . . **and**, reaching work late, **was** warned . . .

'Which' serving two verbs

Exercise 139

1. I want to study maths which will be useful to me and the university will require for my degree.
2. Mother bought Mary a lovely pony which is both her birthday and her Christmas present and certainly she will exercise every day.
3. He does not like cabbage which is a pity and the doctors say will harm his health.

4. I expected him to take home the shield which was his, as winner of the race, to hold for a year.
5. My relatives bought Elsie a wonderful present which was a great pleasure for me to see.
6. The author told me about his new book which was obvious he wanted me to buy.
7. We have a new computer which my brother and I can use and might be available for others as well.
8. Grandmother likes her cup of tea which she takes with lemon and keeps her going all the afternoon.

Comment
'Which' cannot be, in one word, both subject and object. Hence:

1. . . . to me and **which** the university . . .
2. . . . present and **which** she will . . .
3. . . . and **which** the doctors say will . . .
4. . . . to hold **it** for the year . . . ('which' cannot be subject of 'was' and object of 'hold' at the same time).
5. . . . which **it** was a great pleasure . . .
6. . . . book which **it** was obvious . . .
7. . . . can use and **which** might be . . .
8. . . . with lemon and **which** keeps her going . . .

The phrase 'in which to . . .'

Exercise 140
1. That is a very fine box in which to keep your money.
2. That is an easy place from which to get away.
3. Is this the place at which the bus stops?
4. Do you know for sure from which town he comes?

5. Did mother tell you for which items to pay when we do the shopping?
6. That is a terrible predicament out of which to get.
7. You should have checked before we started in which direction to go.
8. Perhaps we should have followed the route by which the old farmer came.

Comment

Echoes of the split infinitive can lead us into strange areas of grammatical pedantry. The English language has a number of verbs which, although they consist of separate words, may signify an indivisible verbal idea. It is easy to point to some of our Germanic linguistic cousins, for example: *aufrufen* is 'to summon', 'to call *up*'; *einnehmen* is 'to receive', 'to take *in*'; *vorgehen* is 'to advance', 'to walk *ahead*'. With this in mind, a strong case is to be made for regarding verbs such as 'to go in', 'to come by', 'to put up', 'to kick off', and many others, as single verbs, deserving to be left free from unnecessary grammatical invasion. Hence:

1. . . . to keep your money in.
2. . . . place to get away from.
3. . . . which the bus stops at.
4. . . . which town he comes from.
5. . . . which items to pay for . . .
6. . . . predicament to get out of.
7. . . . which direction to go in.
8. . . . which the old farmer came by.

Confusion between 'which', 'that' and 'who'

Exercise 141

1. The Albert Hall that is a great Victorian shrine stages many different events during the year.

2. A dog, which obviously had been injured in the crash, was being nursed by a vet.
3. The young girl which was chosen to be May Queen was very nervous.
4. My Uncle Bill that came to dinner at Christmas was always very kind to me.
5. Any policeman who is on patrol duty knows that stray dogs can be a menace.
6. John Smithers, the scientist, that is visiting London tomorrow, will address the meeting.
7. Challenger II that the Americans launched last week landed safely this morning.
8. The town which I would most like to live in is Sydney, Australia.

Comment

For general rules:

1. **which** should be used for non-defining and **that** for defining clauses.
2. **which** refers to things and **who** to persons.
3. **who** is better for particular persons and **that** for a general class of persons.

Thus:

1. The Albert Hall, which . . . shrine, stages . . . (non-defining)
2. A dog that obviously . . . (no comma after 'crash') (defining)
3. The young girl who . . . ('who', not 'which')
4. My Uncle Bill, who . . . Christmas, was . . . ('who', not 'that')
5. Any policeman that is . . . (generic)
6. . . . the scientist, who . . . (particular)

7. Challenger II, which . . . week, landed . . . (non-defining)
8. The town that . . . (defining).

'Which' after a superlative

Exercise 142
1. John Bowles was one of the best hurdlers which Great Britain had produced in the last five years.
2. The most exciting book which I have ever read is 'The Thirty-Nine Steps'.
3. She was a wonderful singer, perhaps the greatest which Italy had ever heard.
4. The last war was the worst which we had experienced in this country.

Comment
Which should not be used after a superlative. Use **that** (which in many sentences can be omitted).

'Which' as a relative adverb

Exercise 143
1. In February we are going to Norway, the earliest time which it has been felt possible to travel so far north.
2. The villain smiled in a way which hinted to the audience he was up to no good.
3. He ran the office in a manner which alienated everyone from manager to filing-clerk.
4. Before the motorways were jammed to the extent which they are now, it was a pleasure to drive along them.
5. The stall-holders were competing for sites in the market in a way which revealed how ruthless they could be over trading rights.

Comment

The **which** clauses in these sentences are defining and attached to such phrases as 'in a way', 'in a manner', 'to the extent', and 'which' cannot be used. Use **that** in each case.

'Which' and 'who' with collective nouns

Exercise 144

1. A large section of the meeting which were in favour of a strike voted against the motion.
2. The mob of soldiers, running in different directions, which were called in by the Governor, fired at the crowd.
3. All that section who is in Block A must go for lunch at 12 noon.
4. The Cyclists' Union, who uses the initials C.A.A., agrees to fund the rally.
5. The team who is picked for Saturday will meet outside the King's Arms.

Comment

If I talk about a *crowd* of people and regard *crowd* as a singular noun, I am talking about a **thing**.

If I talk about a *crowd* of people and regard *crowd* as a number of individual persons, I am talking about **people**.

Under Exercise 141, Rule 2, we use **who** for people and **which** for things.

Therefore:

1. . . . section of the people **who** were in favour . . .
2. The mob . . . **who** were called in . . .
3. All that section **which** is in . . . (or **who are** in . . .)

4. The Cyclists' Union, **which** uses . . .
5. The team **which** is . . . (or **that** is . . .)

'WHO'

'Who' and 'that'

Exercise 145
1. It was he that did it.
2. All who came late will be fined.
3. No one who has a cold will be allowed to go.
4. Anyone who has not washed his hands cannot have lunch.
5. I sat next to Lord Topman, that had come to give the address.
6. The most exciting lady present was Jill, who had flown in from Hollywood.
7. Among the visitors was my cousin, that was recovering from a bad accident.
8. The ladies that came to the party really enjoyed themselves.

Comment
It would be convenient to think that in all defining clauses, whether qualifying persons or things, **that** was the recommended relative and in non-defining clauses **who** was used for persons and **which** for things.

That, however, is used for persons with some reluctance and, whatever grammar may say, vestiges of courtesy and even chivalry haunt the way we use our words. Compare, for example,

The children that (who?) were playing . . .
The hero that (whom?) everyone acclaimed . . .

Note: Words like 'it', 'all', 'no one', 'anyone' are usually followed by *that*.

1. It was he **who** did it.
2. Admissible sentence, but also: All **that** came late . . .
3. No one **that** has a cold . . .
4. Correct sentence.
5. . . . Lord Topman, **who** had . . .
6. Correct sentence.
7. . . . my cousin, **who** was recovering . . .
8. The ladies **who** came . . .

'Who' and 'whom'

Exercise 146
1. There is the man who, some years ago, we knew as George Henry Woods.
2. Jim discovered that many friends who in former days he had trusted now refused to talk to him.
3. We have a difficult decision to make as to whom is to captain the side on Monday.
4. The little girl who had already said whom was to come to her party began to write out the invitations.
5. The staff chose as Head Boy Paul Smith, whom they had just congratulated on his excellent exam results and was also captain of both soccer and cricket XIs.
6. The butcher refused to serve the customer whom, he said, was very rude to him.
7. The police depended on the evidence of Mrs Smith whom, they had believed, knew more about the robbery than anyone else.
8. Who did you go to the film with last night?

Comment

When using these relatives, be scrupulous about the correct case:

Who = Nominative
Whom = Accusative

One proviso is that colloquial practice often sanctions doubtful grammar. We do not object in speech to

Who did you get that from?

but such liberties ought not to be taken in writing, unless we are using dialogue. Where the grammatically correct alternative seems too pedantic, a fresh construction will provide an answer.

1. . . . the man **whom** . . . we knew . . .
2. . . . many friends **whom** . . . he had trusted . . .
3. . . . as to **who** is to captain . . .
4. . . . who had already said **who** was to come . . .
5. . . . exam results and **who** was . . . (the relative must be repeated as it requires a different form)
6. . . . the customer **who** . . . was rude to him.
7. . . . Mrs Smith **who** . . . knew more about . . .
8. Colloquially admissible. Grammatically, 'whom' is correct, or: **Which friend** did you go . . .

'Who' and 'whom' with person and number

Exercise 147
1. To you, who has been given a medal, my exploits will seem prosaic.
2. Ronald did not even notice me who, after all, has been so close to him over the years.
3. For me, who has worked so hard for peace, the threat of war was alarming.

4. The teacher did not even suggest that you, who has always been top of the class, should have a prize.
5. I who, whatever they like to say, has scored more runs than anyone else, should have been asked to play for the county.
6. The death of P.C. Coleman deprives us of one of the few policemen whose reputation places him above the level of ordinary people.
7. Bill Edwards, one of the miners who was killed in the accident, leaves a widow and three children.

Relative pronouns inherit the gender and number of their antecedents. Singulars and plurals must be followed strictly, as well as gender relationships. Thus:

1. To you, who **have** been . . . (you have)
2. . . . notice me . . . who **have** been . . . (I have been)
3. For me, who **have** worked . . . (I have worked)
4. . . . that you, who **have always** . . .
5. I who . . . **have** scored . . .
6. . . . whose reputation places **them** . . . (policemen)
7. . . . the miners who **were** killed . . .

'WHOSE'

Exercise 148
1. I enjoyed listening to the Mozart quartet, in which the inventiveness of the counterpoint was a delight.
2. Harry installed a new lamp of which the brilliance lit up the whole of his garden.
3. The House was debating the Laundry Bill, of which the difficulties were made worse by the

language it was written in.
4. Poor old Fido slept in a kennel of which the roof was full of cracks and holes.
5. The councillor proposed a new scheme, of which the details were contained in a long appendix.

Comment

There is no need to be reluctant to use **whose** when referring to inanimate antecedents. The following corrections are quite acceptable:

1. . . . quartet, the inventiveness of **whose** counterpoint was . . .
2. . . . a lamp, **whose** brilliance . . .
3. . . . Bill, **whose** difficulties . . .
4. . . . kennel **whose** roof . . .
5. . . . scheme, **whose** details . . .

'WHO EVER' AND 'WHOEVER'

These can be tricky. 'Whoever', as one word, is a *relative pronoun*, so that it cannot be used, as one word, in a simple sentence. The two parts, 'who' and 'ever', should rightly be separated.

Exercise 149

Consider these sentences.

1. Whoever knocked at the door?
2. Who ever was here last night?
3. Whoever could have left that bag in the hall?
4. Whomever you said was responsible must own up.
5. He told whoever he saw in the street about his good fortune.

6. The man questioned whomever he saw near the accident.
7. To whomever he spoke he had a cheery word.
8. He was grateful to whoever gave him a donation.

Comment

When 'whoever' appears in a relative clause, its case is decided by that clause, not by the main clause.

Note the forms: nominative: whoever, whosoever, whoe'er (poetic)
accusative: whomever, whoever (colloquial)

Hence:

1. No relative clause. Write: **Who ever** knocked . . .
2. Sentence correct.
3. Better: **Who** could **ever** have left . . .
4. **Whoever** . . . was responsible (nominative)
5. . . . **whomever** he saw . . . (accusative)
6. Sentence correct.
7. Sentence correct; 'whomever' object of 'to'.
8. Sentence correct.

'THAN'

'Than' after certain verbs

Exercise 150
Consider these sentences.

1. I much prefer whisky than sherry.
2. I prefer to dance to swimming.
3. We would prefer to pay teachers more money than to have larger classes.

4. He said he would prefer the Moderate Party to govern the country than the Progressives.
5. The doctor would prefer to have the hospital's report than to prescribe without it.
6. The children had hardly started their sandwiches than they were surrounded by a flock of birds.
7. The school bell had scarcely rung than the teacher appeared in the playground.
8. Hardly had the boat docked than the gangway was lowered and the passengers alighted.
9. The women were in favour of buying sausage rolls for the buffet rather than make sandwiches for so many people.
10. The champion was confident of winning the next set rather than lose it to an unseeded player.

Comment

A. The idiom is 'prefer **to**'. 'Prefer **than**' is wrong.
B. We can change the verb to 'choose', but if we wish to retain 'prefer', we must use '**rather than**'.
C. 'Hardly' and 'scarcely than' must be avoided. Use '**when**'. 'No sooner than' is acceptable.
D. 'Than' prefers the gerund to the infinitive.

Hence:

1. I much prefer whisky **to** sherry.   (A)
2. I prefer to dance **rather** than to swim (or) I prefer **dancing** to swimming.   (B)
3. . . .   more   money   rather   than   **have** larger . . .   (B)
4. . . . the country rather than the Progressives. (B)
5. . . . report **rather than** prescribe . . .   (B)
6. . . . their sandwiches **when** they were . . .   (C)
7. . . . scarcely rung **when** the teacher . . .   (C)

8. . . . the boat docked **when** the gangway . . .   (C)
9. . . . rather than **making** sandwiches . . .   (D)
10. . . . rather than **losing** it . . .   (D)

'Than' as conjunction and preposition

Exercise 151
1. The test match was rained off and no one regretted it more than us.
2. The assistant in the clothes department was more helpful than her in the toy department.
3. As the opposing company have more resources than us we must give in.
4. I am leaving the City Choir and shall join the Royal Choir, because their singers are better than us.
5. I hope I get more pudding than him because I am so hungry.
6. They will never engage a better striker than him who scored that second goal.
7. Mabel had no kinder friend than her whom she had known since childhood.
8. The country never had better leaders than they who the Germans so badly underestimated during World War II.

Comment
Consider these sentences.

A. You love her more than I love her
B. You love her more than I
C. You love her more than me.

A. **Than** is a subordinating adverbial conjunction linking 'more' with 'I love her'. The meaning is clear.

B. If we are to understand that 'love her' has been left out, then **than** is the same as in A, and so is the meaning.

C. This sentence is ambiguous, it can have two meanings.

1. You love her more than you love me.
2. You love her more than I love her. (me = colloquial form of 'I')

Here, **than** is a subordinating conjunction (1) or a co-ordinating conjunction (2). The reader has to interpret the meaning from the context.

To parse **than** as a preposition, governing 'me', in the sense that 'You love her more than you love me' is regarded as incorrect. This is an academic point. The meaning is usually clear from the context, but sentences such as these are regarded as flawed.

Hence:

1. . . . regretted it more than **we** (did).
2. . . . more helpful than **she** (is) in the toy . . .
3. . . . more resources than **we** (have), we must . . .
4. . . . are better than **we** (are)
5. . . . more pudding than **he** (gets).
6. . . . better striker than **he** (is) who scored . . .
7. . . . friend than **she** (is) whom . . .
8. . . . leaders than **they** correct **whom** the Germans . . .

[If the words in brackets are included, confusion is avoided.]

MISCELLANY

'Between'

1. **Between** must be followed by

   A plural word *or*
   two separate expressions joined by 'and'.

   These are wrong:
   Tom went to the toilet between every lesson.
       (between lessons)
   There must be no argument between each member of the team.
       (between each member and other members or between them)
2. Always write between you and me
                        you and him
                        me and her
                        us and them (all accusative)
3. Do not repeat *between*:
       I'll meet you between Tower Bridge and between London Bridge. (wrong)
4. Do not use 'between . . . or . . .'
       The vicar was torn between visiting Mrs Cook, who was very poorly, or opening the craft fair at the hall. (Wrong – **and** opening the craft fair . . .)

'Both . . . And'

These words should be followed by arrangements of words that are grammatically equivalent. E.g.

He played in **both** the football team **and** the cricket team.

He played **both** **in** the football team **and** **in** the cricket team.

Note:

He played in **both** the football **and** cricket teams. (wrong)

Both the biscuits **and** cakes were quickly eaten. (wrong)

Both the biscuits **and** the cakes were . . . (correct)

'But'

This word is still regarded as a preposition in some circumstances (but = except).

I want you to give it to no one but **him**.
It is known to everyone but **her**.

Note: 'No one cares but me' is wrong. This should be 'No one cares but I (care).' **But** is a conjunction here, not a preposition. Hence:

No one goes there but I (go there). (This can be 'me', colloquially.) It can be reasoned that **but** in this sentence is a preposition (= except). Whatever choice is made, you should be aware of the grammar.

'Due to'/'Owing to'

'Due to' is used in an adjectival sense; e.g.

1. Something that ought to be given to a person/thing.
   'Give the landlord the rent that is due to him.'

2. In the sense of 'Can be ascribed to'.
   'His illness was due to exposure to radiation for such a long time.'

As an adjective, 'due to' must be attached to a noun or pronoun.

'I am due to attend court tomorrow.'
'The non-appearance of the train was due to **engine failure**.'

'Owing to' is a compound preposition, sometimes interchangeable with 'due to':

'The aircraft returned to base **due to** (**owing to**) a technical fault.'
but not always:
'My flat is uninhabitable owing to dampness and dry rot.'

Avoid 'owing to the fact that'; use 'because'.

In the following examples, 'because of' would be preferable.

1. The hockey team is to disband owing to the lack of leadership from Mr Smith.
2. It was due to Mr Smith's failure as a leader that the hockey team had to disband.
3. Deer, owing to the fact that they are constantly being hunted, flee as soon as they see a man.
4. It is due to man's appetite for hunting that the deer flee from his sight.
5. Coffee has increased in price owing to the demand from Europe.
6. Due to Europe's demand for more coffee, it has increased in price.

Indirect Questions

'Who are these men?' 'Where are the boys going?' 'Have the goods arrived?' are **direct questions**. If I report these questions to someone else, I must modify their form:

I asked him *who the men were*.
He told me *where the boys were going*.
I wondered *if the goods had arrived*.

As they are no longer direct questions but **indirect** questions, they do not need the punctuation device.

The words in italics in the full sentences are the equivalent of a noun and thus to be regarded as a noun in the singular. Hence:

Who these men were **was** a mystery to all of us.
Where the boys were going after lunch **was** still to be decided.
If the goods had arrived **was** the question the boss was asking.

'The'

The repetition of **the** with expressions of several adjectives or nouns is often a matter of nice judgment rather than grammatical compulsion.

There is an obvious difference between 'the red and white balloons' and 'the red and the white balloons' and a careful writer will observe this difference. However, there will be occasions when the omission of the second (or third, or fourth) **the** is acceptable, if not actually necessary.

'THE' WITH TWO NOUNS AND A SINGULAR VERB

Consider:

The wit and wisdom of Bernard Shaw is (are) well-known to all his readers.

Many writers will feel that 'wit' and 'wisdom', although separate ideas, here form one entity and so tolerate a singular verb.

His wit and wisdom **is** well known.

In fact, the single 'is' strengthens the force of the double subject and makes it more idiomatic. Care, however, should be taken to ensure that the double subject is a legitimate single idea.

The strain and stress is . . . (Yes)

The joy and pleasure of the occasion was . . .
  (Possibly)

The charm and intelligence of the man was . . .
  (Never; use 'were')

'This', 'That', 'These', 'Those'

In phrases such as 'these boys listed', 'those people mentioned', 'this plan specified', 'that girl described', the words 'boys', 'people', 'plan' and 'girl' already have adjectives qualifying their meaning:

'boys *listed*', 'people *mentioned*', 'plan *specified*', 'girl *described*'. They do not require a *demonstrative* adjective further pointing to them. The phrases should read:

'**the** people mentioned', '**the** boys listed', etc.

'Those kind'

'Those kind of things . . .' – in conversation can be forgiven but, in writing, they are always, '**those kinds**'. Similarly, of course, '**those sorts**'.

i.e. and e.g.

i.e. should be used to provide another way of saying what has already been said, not to introduce an example.

> The sign said you must not cross the railway lines to reach the other platform; i.e. you should use the footbridge.

> **e.g.** introduces an example; e.g.

> I looked for some more materials, e.g. silks, satins or cottons, to complete the collage.

i.e. and e.g. should be preceded by a stop, but whether a comma is placed after them is not grammatically important.

Index

Notes

Notes